The
Higher Education

The Future of Higher Education

Edited by Tom Schuller

The Society for Research into Higher Education
& Open University Press

Published by SRHE and
Open University Press
Celtic Court
22 Ballmoor
Buckingham
MK18 1XW

and

1900 Frost Road, Suite 101
Bristol, PA 19007, USA

First Published 1991

British Library Cataloguing in Publication Data

The future of higher education. – (SRHE/Open University Press series)
  I. Schuller, Tom   II. Series
  378.0941

  ISBN 0–335–09794–4
  ISBN 0–335–09793–6 pbk

Library of Congress Cataloging-in-Publication Number Available

Typeset by Graphicraft Typesetters Ltd., Hong Kong
Printed in Great Britain by St Edmundsbury Press Ltd,
Bury St Edmunds, Suffolk

Contents

List of Contributors

Sir Christopher Ball
Royal Society of Arts

Tessa Blackstone
Master, Birkbeck College

Colin Flint
Principal, Solihull College of Technology

Andrew McPherson
Director, Centre for Educational Sociology, University of Edinburgh

Pauline Perry
Director, South Bank Polytechnic

Elizabeth Reid
Deputy Provost, City of London Polytechnic

Michael Richardson
Director and Secretary, Board of Extra-Mural Studies, University of
Cambridge (formerly Pro-Vice Chancellor, Open University)

Tom Schuller
Director, Centre for Continuing Education, University of Edinburgh

Peter Scott
Editor, *Times Higher Education Supplement*

Michael Shattock
Registrar, University of Warwick

William H. Stubbs
Chief Executive, Polytechnics and Colleges Funding Council

Gareth Williams
Director, Centre for Higher Education Studies, Institute of Education,
London University

Acknowledgements

Several thanks are due: to the Leverhulme Trust for financing the reassessment; to Gareth Williams, Tessa Blackstone, Christopher Ball, Oliver Fulton, Peter Scott and Michael Shattock for their advice on the project; to Jenny Jedrej for her indefatigable assistance in the preparation of the seminar; to Cari Loder for her particular help in its management; to Anne Marie Bostyn for her help in preparing the manuscript; and to Birkbeck College for its hospitality.

Abbreviations

ABRC	Advisory Board for the Research Councils
BTEC	Business and Technician Education Council
CDP	Committee of Directors and Principals
CIHE	Council for Industry in Higher Education
CNAA	Council for National Academic Awards
CPS	Centre for Policy Studies
CVCP	Committee of Vice-Chancellors and Principals
DES	Department of Education and Science
EHE	Enterprise in Higher Education
HMI	Her Majesty's Inspectorate
IPPR	Institute for Public Policy Research
NAB	National Advisory Board
NAFE	Non-advanced Further Education
NVQ	National Vocational Qualification
OECD	Organization for Economic Co-operation and Development
PICKUP	Professional Industrial and Commercial Updating
PCFC	Polytechnics and Colleges Funding Council
PSI	Policy Studies Institute
SCOTVEC	Scottish Vocational Education Council
SED	Scottish Education Department
SRHE	Society for Research into Higher Education
TEC	Training and Enterprise Councils
UFC	Universities Funding Council
UGC	University Grants Committee

1

Reassessing the Future

Tom Schuller

Background note

This volume has something of a Janus-like character. It was conceived of as
a reassessment of the study bearing the same name, carried out over roughly
a three-year period at the turn of the last decade. That study, jointly
sponsored by the Society for Research into Higher Education (SRHE) and
the Leverhulme Trust, was and is the most substantial review of higher
education policy since the Robbins Report in 1963. It was based on substantial fresh research; covered a wide range of issues in its eleven volumes; and
offered a large number of recommendations, summarized in the last two
volumes, *Response to Adversity* (Williams and Blackstone 1983) and *Excellence in
Diversity* (SRHE-Leverhulme 1983). Its analysis and recommendations had
not been exhausted as the 1980s drew to a close. The reassessment was
designed to look back over the intervening period and offer a view on the
validity and effect of FHE1 (as the first study will be called); and at the same
time to look forward and offer an agenda for higher education for the
forthcoming decade. The Janus profile is not symmetrical, for the volume
concentrates heavily on the future, as its name implies. Itemized retrospection
is left largely to Gareth Williams, the director of FHE1, in Chapter 2, though
all the authors have contributed with an awareness, often explicit, of the
perspective furnished by the reassessment.

The structure of FHE2 (as this volume will be called) has been built
around three themes: *access, governance* and *quality*. In selecting these I was
conscious of the obvious fact that important elements of FHE1 would be
simply excluded. Research and the arts, for example, are not explicitly
addressed as separate issues in their own right. But the three themes reflect,
in a way that pays tribute to the first study, the extent to which its eventual
main themes remain current priorities – even though the terms themselves
now carry a slightly different set of meanings and resonances (exploration of
these differences being part of the reassessment).

As for the mechanics of FHE2, for each theme two authors were asked to
prepare a brief paper. These were presented at a seminar which provided a

focal point for the reassessment, and subsequently expanded in the light of the discussion there. (A list of the participants is provided as the Appendix.)[1] Additional papers are included from Tessa Blackstone, who collaborated with Gareth Williams in directing FHE1, and Colin Flint. The inclusion of the latter is of specific significance since it represents the acceptance of further education into this debate, perhaps the single most striking contrast with FHE1; this point is picked up in several of the chapters. The collection is completed by contributions from Peter Scott, Michael Shattock and Sir Christopher Ball. All of these were centrally involved in FHE1, and acted as convenors of the three main themes at the FHE2 seminar; their contributions are personal views, but are fashioned out of the group discussions which took place there.

The collection does not purport to be comprehensive. There is, for example, no student point of view, nor any from the school sector, though Andrew Collier, President of the Society of Education Officers, contributed to the conclusions articulated in the final session of the focal seminar. It may appear unduly insular, though again the seminar welcomed representation from both the European Community (EC) and the Organization for Economic Co-operation and Development. Readers must judge for themselves how serious are these and other omissions; the purpose has been to identify priority areas for debate.

From demand to supply

In his introduction to the early volumes of the previous *Future of Higher Education* study – FHE1 – Gareth Williams presented as 'the fundamental question' confronting higher education 'the extent to which consensual arrangements and assumptions that generally worked well during the long postwar period of its expansion can cope with the much more stringent conditions likely to prevail in the 1980s and 1990s.' A decade later that question as it was then construed has been answered, in the negative; the question now is whether a new consensus can be constructed, at least on the major issues for the future and perhaps also on the priorities for action. Can we manage, as Sir Claus Moser urged in his 1990 presidential address to the British Association, a medium and long term view on education, with at least an element of the visionary in it (Moser 1990)?

The original consensus has been ruptured in part because of the particular ideology of the government which held power during the 1980s, with its hostility towards the public sector as a whole and its determination to introduce market forces wherever possible into the delivery of services. This, along with the restriction of public expenditure, has been the major impulse behind the changes in higher education, crudely yet powerfully accelerating the reconsideration of fundamental assumptions initiated in FHE1. Even had the attitude of government been different, a reappraisal would have been necessary. By dint of sheer repetition if nothing else, the restricted nature of higher education in the UK compared with other industrial nations has become a matter of national concern. There is now unanimity across the political spectrum on the need for a quantum jump in the numbers of people to be given access to it (Chapter 3 gives details of the various projections). The shape that the expansion will take, the way it is to be financed and the values it exhibits remain to be decided.

The consensus on expansion does not extend to how much public money should be put into it, beyond the truism that it must be affordable by the public purse. Underfunding is certainly a key issue, especially in relation to physical plant. Extra resources are desperately needed if Britain is to be able to face the next century with any confidence. But securing extra money will not of itself enable higher education to meet the challenges in front of it. It may not appear so, for instance from the pictures of students sleeping on floors because they cannot afford to pay the rents demanded for decent accommodation, but on a per capita basis students in the UK are far more generously treated than in any other country, in the contact they have with teaching staff and in the level of public contribution to their study and maintenance costs. The expansion recommended by Lord Robbins in 1963 could accommodate, without reform of the structure of higher education, the funding arrangements proposed the year before by the Anderson Committee, enabling students to enjoy residential higher education with buildings and grants provided by government money. But even had the British economy performed substantially better than it has done since, another quantum increase in student numbers on the same unit cost basis as prevailed in the 1960s and 1970s is not a likely prospect.

Quite justifiably, the British system has always had its admirers, for its rapid and high completion rates, linked to the low student-staff ratios. It is safe to say that no country is completely happy with its higher education system, for different reasons, and mere breast-beating is easy but useless. But the question of whether the output from the system is suited to modern times is prompted by a number of factors, not least among them contact with our European neighbours. In the British case there is a well-established shortage of graduates in certain areas, especially scientific and technological. Secondly, one of the key issues identified here and in subsequent chapters is whether the preoccupation with honours graduates is appropriate. Certainly the most apparent shortages are at higher technician rather than honours graduate level; in the latter area the UK does unusually well in international comparisons. On top of this has come speculation as to whether those graduates that do emerge are as well equipped as they might be, personally and occupationally. Here ideology re-enters, for some of this scepticism has voiced itself under the banner of Enterprise in Higher Education, a title redolent of the Conservative government's wider socio-political aspirations. But once the capital E of Enterprise is reduced to normal size, many people would subscribe to the notion that higher education should concern itself more than it has done with the broad skills needed for positive participation in the broad sense (Tolley 1990).

Finally, the expansion of higher education has done little to affect the pattern of its social distribution. Despite the growth of courses specifically tailored to promoting the participation of under-represented groups, public provision in this area, even more than in other social policy fields, has remained overwhelmingly the preserve of the young and the middle classes. The representation of women has increased, albeit not evenly across subjects; but adults over the age of 25, the lower social classes and ethnic minorities are still substantially under-represented, especially in universities. Despite some progress (see Glennerster and Low 1991) incremental expansion has not redressed the massively regressive character of social expenditure on higher education.

The key question towards which all of these factors point is intimidatingly simple: *what is higher education?* The single most important switch of focus needed in higher education policy-making is from *demand* to *supply*. This may appear surprising in the light of the agreed case for a quantum expansion. Yet to proceed on the basis that the central issue is how to expand the existing system, whether for predominantly social or economic reasons, would be to close off crucial areas of debate. Not only is demand itself a function of supply, in the sense that more people try to enter higher education if they perceive that there are places available (see Chapter 3); more importantly still, the value to the individual and to society depends crucially on the nature of what is offered. Is it fit, to use a term currently much in vogue, for the purposes identified by Robbins – meeting the needs of individuals as citizens and workers, and those of society for scholarship, skills and socialization?[2] The answer must be, not fully fit. As long as higher education is interpreted predominantly in terms of full-time, specialized honours degrees we shall never manage to square the circle of both increasing and satisfying demand whilst at the same time assuring high quality. As the title of the influential RSA report has it, more means different (Ball 1990).

The single most striking contrast between FHE1 and FHE2 is the change in levels of demand. At the beginning of the 1980s there was serious talk of having to close some universities for lack of students. Now, as both Williams (Chapter 2) and Scott (Chapter 5) observe, demand is extremely buoyant in spite of the demographic decline in the numbers of young people and the deterioration in some aspects of the quality of academic life, such as staff– student ratios, accommodation of all kinds and levels of student finance. It would be unwise to rely blindly on this buoyancy being maintained, but the numbers of young people will begin to rise again in the mid-1990s, and we now have the built-in motor of higher levels of parental education, which have a direct effect on the next generation's demand patterns. The question, therefore, is not the simple one of how to attract sufficient numbers of students, but how to ensure that the right education is on offer to all potential beneficiaries. This is the dominant theme of the volume.

Once again, FHE1 struck the right note, with the title of its concluding volume, *Excellence in Diversity*, but it looks as if at least a further decade will pass before we can claim to have put this slogan into practice. Access is not only about creating more routes into existing provision, as it is largely interpreted in most universities, but about changing the character of the provision so that it offers a full range of entry and exit points, and a full variety of educational modes, most notably in the provision of part-time opportunities. Whilst polytechnics generally are more flexible in their provision, they cannot in practice operate freely as long as the system favours the traditional model as heavily as it does, without severely risking the quality of what they deliver. And – to complete the trio of both sectors and themes – the governance of the system can only effectively meet the challenge if it embraces further education (FE) institutions which do not themselves deliver degrees.

Whether or not further education comes to be formally classified as part of higher education is not the issue here (see Chapter 9). The second fundamental difference between FHE1 and FHE2 is the acceptance that higher education should not be considered in isolation from the rest of the post-compulsory system (nor, indeed, from the compulsory system itself). A recent report from the Institute for Public Policy Research calls for an end to the division between education and training, with a proposal for 16–19 year olds characterized by 'late selection and high participation' (Finegold *et al.* 1990, p. 6). The same principle could well be applied to higher education. Such an extension of the scope of the debate is only one of a number of ways in which the insularity of higher education has been definitively ruptured. To a greater or lesser extent, the boundaries with government, with industry and with EC countries have all become more permeable, as well as that with further education. Except perhaps for the first, there is little cause for regret in this.

It is crucial that the changes implicit in this reorientation be seen in the context of expansion. It is balance that is at issue. We are not talking about dismembering the degree system and scattering its parts about in some modularized maelstrom. The argument is that the transition from elite to mass higher education entails a genuine reshaping of the system and not an inflation of it which preserves its current proportions, like a balloon blown up bigger. Existing modes will have their place within the new shape, but they will, in relative terms, occupy less space.

One way of illustrating this is to focus for a moment on the indicators of expansion. At present, the key indicator used is the Age Participation Rate (APR), the proportion of a given cohort of young people who proceed to higher education. (An alternative, more sophisticated, measure is the Qualified Participation Index, which takes into account the proportions of school leavers conventionally qualified for higher education; see Chapter 3 for an account of this and other measures.) This is based on two assumptions: first, that entry into higher education is in effect concerned with school leavers, and secondly that entry into higher education is the key issue, rather than what goes on in it. The latter assumption is justified, from one point of view, by the very high completion rates of the British system, with very few students, once enrolled, failing to complete their degree. But a more appropriate way of measuring participation would challenge both assumptions. First, it would include some measure of adult enrolments, instead of concentrating on the cohort of young people. Secondly, it would place much more emphasis than at present on differentiating between enrolments at different levels within the system, switching attention from entry to exit points. The central measurement would then be of the numbers (or proportions) attaining different levels of higher education.

Something of the kind is provided in *More Means Different*, which set the following targets (Ball 1990, p. 26).

Raise ASPIRATIONS	>>					
Provide OPPORTUNITIES	3–5	5–11	11–16	16–18	18–21	21+
Set targets for PARTICIPATION	100%	100%	100%	90%	60%	(100% at least a fortnight per year)
Set targets for ACHIEVEMENT	(motivated to learn)	(100% literacy)	95% NVQ2	85% NVQ3	30% NVQ4 30% NVQ5	all raise level of attainment at least one grade
Assess and evaluate ENABLEMENT	>>					

This gives a clear guide to the desired future shape of the system, with the proportions expected to complete different levels of attainment. It needs to be complemented by a measure which might be called the Population Participation Index (PPI), which would tell us amongst other things how many of those who left education some time ago are returning to study. Obviously this figure would as a proportion be only a small fraction of the APR. But if we are to make lifelong learning a reality, we need some measure of this kind. With a population of adults over 25 which is currently some 37 million, we might aim for a gross PPI of 3 per cent annually.[3] Many of these would not be participating in degrees; some would have a degree already, and they and others would be returning for shorter courses (though one should not assume that people would not wish to do a second degree). Not every instance of participation could be recorded for the purposes of the PPI – perhaps only those that formed part of a qualification with a minimum length of study. But it would certainly give us a better idea of how well higher education was serving the needs of the population as a whole, and would force a more fine-meshed assessment of quantitative performance.

To sum up the argument so far:

1. Whilst the original purposes specified by Robbins for higher education can still be accepted as broad guidelines, they need substantial reinterpretation if they are to be applied to the future system.

2. A shift in focus to the supply side raises a host of issues about fitness for purpose. Expanded demand cannot necessarily be assumed, though the signs are promising, unlike at the time of FHE1. The needed expansion will depend on what is offered as much on factors such as levels of parental education and school performance.
3. An expanded system should assume a different shape from the current one: a smaller role for full-time specialized degrees, with a finer grading of opportunities offering greater variety of exit as well as entry points.
4. Further education should be regarded as an integral part of the policy debate on higher education.
5. We need to adopt a different basic system for measuring participation in higher education, capturing the requisite variety of provision and including the population as a whole.

Themes and issues

I turn now to the specific themes identified as central: access, governance and quality. I shall offer first a brief overview of the arguments presented in the chapters which follow, adding in points made in the focal seminar. I shall then discuss three issues which to differing degrees cut across these themes. In each case there is a balance between an institutional and a system focus, and between the university and the polytechnic and college sectors.

Access

In a sense, as Scott observes (Chapter 5), access now has primacy of place, but with a different meaning to that attributed to it a decade ago. It is no longer a question of providing entry points for more people, especially for those from under-represented social groups. It concerns the structure of the edifice they enter. To continue the architectural metaphor: whereas before the primary concern was with fitting more doors, and even windows, it is now with redesigning the interior, giving it more storeys with lower ceilings and more sets of stairs between them. Tenants who come in and out on a daily basis (as part-time students) must be given full rights of residence, as in Blackstone's case study of Birkbeck College (Chapter 12). Substantial extension is required to the ground floor (the initial stage of higher education).

Both McPherson (Chapter 3) and Reid (Chapter 4) address directly the relationship between increased and wider access. (Scott uses a similar distinction, but expresses it as access versus Access.) Increased access is to do with numbers, wider access with their social distribution. Significantly, they agree that increased access should be given priority, without this entailing an abandonment of the commitment to widening access. Here is a key shift in emphasis. It is a challenge to those concerned about the distributive aspects of higher education to take their arguments into the mainstream of the debate, and not to be implicitly content with a redistribution of opportunity in a zero sum game. Reid's acceptance of increased access as a precondition for wider access is followed by a set of thoroughly practical guidelines for institutional managers to ensure that wider access is indeed achieved.

McPherson draws on the example of Scotland to show how much more has been achieved in one region of what is thought of as a British system. Amongst other factors the availability of finely graded options for achievement at school encourages a significantly higher staying on rate and consequently an entry rate into higher education which is already close to targets which the rest of the UK is struggling to accept for the end of the decade. He extends the logic of the argument to suggest that we might reconceptualize higher education in terms of stages rather than levels. Targets for wider access must be expressed in terms of outflows from groups, not simply in terms of inflows to institutions, and the idea of 'access' must be extended from its present focus on initial entry to comprehend some notion of sustained and successful participation. The potential for higher education is not dichotomous but continuous; in other words, it is not a question of whether or not a person can benefit, but how much, at any given stage.

Scott and Reid both maintain the validity of enlightened self-interest as a motive for institutions to concern themselves with wider access. But the downgrading of the role of local authorities may well have weakened the drive for greater social equality. Without their influence, institutions have less incentive to set themselves objectives on this score. There is a further fear. Despite Flint's bullish tone in Chapter 9, further education will have to struggle to assert its claims in the wider arena of local authority priority-setting, given its non-statutory status. There is a looming irony here, that the growing recognition of the crucial role of further education in expanding access may be accompanied by a dismantling of the instruments needed to give effective support for that role. The recent White Papers relating to FE (DES 1991; SOED 1991) whilst promoting its vocational profile do nothing to allay such fears.

McPherson and Scott give different lists of factors influencing demand, ranging from the structure of school examinations through parental levels of education to general levels of wealth. Whatever the different weightings that may be attributed to the various factors, it is the supply of opportunities – quantitative and qualitative, for school leavers and for other age groups – that is crucial.

Governance

Perhaps the most important single issue to emerge from the discussions of governance is that of accountability. This is most aptly illustrated in the currency of mission statements. Mission statements have prompted a good deal of cynicism, and as Stubbs observes in Chapter 6, speaking from a position of sectoral responsibility, they will no longer be permitted to remain as bland descriptions of the future; instead they will become key indicators of institutional performance. Richardson (Chapter 7) similarly queries the credibility of some of the statements that have been issued, and asks how and by whom the institution's adherence to its statement will be judged.

The existence of the binary line, dividing universities from polytechnics, provokes less agonizing here than in FHE1.[4] Nevertheless, what might be called the division of institutional labour is a major issue confronting those working at different levels. Richardson refers to the blurring of boundaries between the sectors, and Stubbs points to the possibility of a restratification of institutions following the allocation of research resources. The fundamental line will not, on this scenario, be between universities, which are funded to do research, and polytechnics which are not, but between different sets of institutions with different mixes of research and teaching, with some doing no research at all. Shattock (Chapter 8) also identifies the problem as being where to draw the line, but suggests that the problem is as much that the line is too hard. In fact, there is not likely to be a single line. The conclusion must be that there will inevitably be differentiation between sets of institutions, and the hard question is how to ensure on the one hand that this is functional and on the other that from the students' viewpoint it does not unnecessarily impede their movement from one sector to another. Such a conclusion may appear inconclusive; it nevertheless reinforces the basic message of greater diversity of provision.

Both Shattock and Richardson explicitly raise the issue of how differentiation and the introduction of a greater market element affect relationships between institutions. Shattock, like Williams, is generally positive about the impact that this has had so far. But along with Richardson he insists that there is a balance to be struck between encouraging competition, for example because it rewards innovation and responsiveness, and yet maintaining the type of collaboration which will make the system work as a system.

Stubbs, although careful to avoid a sectarian stance, suggests the possibility that universities may become a minority player in the expansionist future that is commonly accepted. The link to access is evident. Universities as a group, or as individual institutions, are faced with a decision about how far they stake a claim to be part of that future, and therefore to accept as well as to influence the changes that come with it. Alongside the redivision of institutional labour comes a redivision of academic labour at the individual level (see pp. 14–17), and it is difficult to see how more than a minority of universities can insulate themselves from the implications of increased access.

Quality

There can be no dispute over the essential message to emerge under this heading. Diversity of provision entails diversity in our notion of quality – hence the title of Ball's overview in Chapter 11. Perry (Chapter 10), speaking as the head of an institution with very diverse functions but also from long experience in HM Inspectorate, is quite explicit that diversity entails inequality. This, it should be stressed, is not the same as accepting low as well as high quality; she is making the point that not all institutions should aspire to qualities of the same kind. Like Williams in his discussion of structure, she uses an analogy with the car industry, suggesting that price is related directly to quality. This observation, however, should be set alongside her reference to fitness for purpose for, as Williams observes, the most expensive product is not necessarily the one best suited to every purpose.

Perry reminds us that new definitions of quality are being derived from industry. Yet there are of course limitations to the applicability of the analogy. The products of higher education cannot be 'controlled' in the same way as the output of a manufacturing plant; if it were so predictable we could hardly claim to be engaged in the business of *education*. Interestingly, the Director of the Council for Higher Education and Industry, Patrick Coldstream, speaking at the FHE2 seminar on the quality theme, urged educationalists to be more boldly philosophical in their approach to the future, and not to confine themselves to attempting to elicit industry's needs. Quality in education must allow for variation, without supposing that there is a single dimension. Perry's chapter takes us painstakingly through the arguments, including the distinction between 'threshold' judgements, which relate to basic quality, and 'premium' judgements which seek to identify performance of unusual standard.

There are links across to the issue of governance, especially in the sphere of accountability. Who is to take responsibility for quality, and how is it to be built in to the system? Perry places considerable emphasis on the role of the head of department, and Blackstone shows how positive decisions must be taken on the allocation of resources in order to maintain and improve quality in straitened economic circumstances. Naturally there is much scope for including the student as a judge of quality. But Perry reminds us that there can be a tension between student perception of needs and wider social perceptions of what higher education should be delivering – for example in obliging engineering students to develop language skills.

Ball provides a model for analysing the different qualities involved and the means for judging them. Driving home the message of plurality, he proposes a triple relativity: to purpose, to previous performance and to the performance of others. With this we are beginning to move away from grand statements of minimal import, and towards a proper framework for judgement – and therefore again for accountability.

Issue one: a different time structure: shorter cycles and an end to full-time versus part-time

My first issue has been well foreshadowed. It is the abandonment of the gold standard of the full-time three- or four-year honours degree in favour of a model based on an initial broader qualification equivalent to two years' full-time study followed by further cycles of one or two years each, covering postgraduate as well as undergraduate study. 'Years' is a risky shorthand; it allows a common temporal currency to exist but loads the dice in favour of full-time education however often one inserts afterwards 'or part-time equivalent'. The 1990s may be the decade when part-time study becomes an acknowledged feature of all higher education, and in particular the vehicle for accommodating significant expansion. A subsidiary concern is the extent to which 'full-time' really means what it says, and whether the academic year needs to be re-examined.

In an earlier retrospective on FHE1, Williams offered the following challenge:

> One generalization I would be prepared to debate is that the basic structure of higher education courses has changed less in Britain in the past quarter century than in any other advanced country. (1985 p. 59)

The arguments for changing the fundamental structure of courses were fully rehearsed in FHE1 (Fulton 1981b); were reiterated in the RSA study (Ball 1990); and are here cogently repeated by Williams in Chapter 2. In brief, they concern:

- the feasibility of substantial expansion
- the correction of excessive specialization
- the promotion of part-time study at different levels
- increasing scope for credit transfer
- better articulation with schools and with the FE sector
- the integration of continuing education into the mainstream of higher education.

I make no apology for developing the argument in a way which overlaps with the chapter by Williams; the duplication signals its primacy.

The relevance to the access theme is obvious, and has already been discussed. Access is not to do only with ways into higher education; it concerns supply as much as demand. If more people are to be attracted into higher education, it cannot be a question of providing more of the same, for two main reasons. First is the matter of resources: there are severe limits on how many more people can be accommodated if they are all to be offered the gold standard version. At its crudest, calculations must be made of the trade-offs between expanding three-year provision and expanding shorter alternatives. Secondly, many more potential students, and especially those from non-traditional backgrounds, are likely to be attracted by shorter courses (all the more so, of course, if the current, in my view wrongheaded, proposals for student loans are further implemented).

The curricular reform involved in establishing a first cycle which gives a broad foundation and allows a better articulation with secondary schooling provides the link with the quality theme. One dimension of quality is to do with fitness for purpose and one purpose of higher education is to provide well trained graduates for public and private sector employment. A more diverse graduate output, with a first cycle which had its own currency, would be fitter (but not, incidentally, leaner; we are, to repeat, setting an expansionist scene). A still stronger argument is that a foundation qualification, properly integrated into a system which allows continuation on to a more specialized further cycle, is better suited to allowing personal development to take place, with greater control over content and timing. The more entry and exit points, the more the individual is able – and required – to make responsible choices, the essential hallmark of personal growth.

The potential flexibility of such a system depends on institutional collaboration, primarily through credit transfer, which is where governance comes in. Credit transfer is less controversial than the abandonment of the gold standard, but there remains the issue of whether it is best implemented through a national initiative or by institutions collaborating bilaterally and multilaterally on an evolving piecemeal basis – or what complementarity can be achieved between initiatives at the two levels. The regional dimension is likely to be important here.

There are a number of arguments which have been put against such a reform, and Scott in this volume expresses his doubts. Some of these have been dealt with in the more general discussion above. Prime amongst them is the view that the proposal means compressing existing degrees into a shorter period and thus reducing the overall student time spent in higher education. I have made it clear that this is a policy for expansion, which does not necessarily involve any reduction in the numbers of those who do three- or four-year degrees.

Other objections are that it would destroy the curricular coherence of the degree, and that it is anyway unnecessary because of the existence of two-year qualifications such as those offered by the Business and Technician Education Council (BTEC) and the Scottish Vocational Education Council (SCOTVEC), and the growth of credit transfer systems. The first would only have weight if it were argued that the foundation degree would simply be a sawn-off version of existing provision; it should be obvious from the above that this is not the case, and that time and resources would need to be devoted to its design and introduction. The notion that there is a fixed quantum of time below which higher education cannot properly be delivered is quite simply implausible. On the other hand, in several disciplines, for example mathematics, physics and engineering, there is now pressure to extend the length of time required to attain honours standard. On its own such an extension is undesirable, reflecting the interests of the academic producer rather than the consumer (student or employer). The introduction of a shorter initial cycle, however, would free the planning of degrees from the constraints imposed by the existing rigid framework. It would also offer an escape from excessive specialization, and by doing so appeal more strongly to mature students, as Blackstone points out.

The second objection fails because it does not address the system as a whole. Whilst piecemeal innovation is effective in some cases, a reform of this kind requires the involvement of all sectors if it is not to suffer from the implicit condemnation of being ignored by high-status institutions. Involvement in the system does not mean that every institution offers the full range of courses. But change at system level means recognition on all sides. In other words, it may be that some institutions – research-oriented universities, for example – would choose not to involve themselves extensively in the delivery of the first cycle. But in so far as they were funded to teach at all, they would be expected to recognize the validity of qualifications gained at that level. The question of the extent to which institutional differentiation should be encouraged is a separate one (see Chapter 6 by Stubbs).

In the United States two-year qualifications are widely available in community colleges, with the possibility of transfer to university. This has allowed mass enrolment in higher education at a variety of points, since direct entry into universities is of course also permitted. The proposal for foundation degrees differs from this model, however, in at least one crucial respect. Whilst the first cycle might well be offered, depending on subject as well as region, in FE colleges, it would be clearly identified as a higher education qualification under the current understanding of that term. It would, in other words, be offered broadly across the system. The American two-year college, for all its merits, has had something of a 'cooling out' effect, discouraging a proportion of students from attempting the second cycle of higher education. A recent study of community colleges describes how they have played the role of 'managing ambition in a society that generates far higher levels of aspiration for upward mobility than it can possibly satisfy,' (Brint and Karabel 1989, p. 213). The proposal here, by contrast, would encourage more people to aspire to higher education. Whilst the tension between the virtues of providing a terminal qualification and the dangers of directly or indirectly discouraging some from proceeding further can never be avoided, a better balance can be achieved which integrates the shorter qualification more fully into the overall system. Integration can be reinforced by requiring institutions to report regularly on the extent to which they are promoting transfer between cycles (Astin 1983).

Finally, there is the argument that there is no evident demand from employers for foundation degrees. It is true that employers will in some cases prefer an honours graduate to a foundation graduate. But there are at least three points to be made here. First, the choice is not between these two categories of potential employee, but between a supply of foundation graduates and a supply of people with no higher education at all; to repeat, it is an expansionary proposition, not a reshuffling of existing numbers. Secondly, provided that the change is genuinely system-wide, and not merely a selection device for segregating different classes of student, employers may well prefer graduates with a broader education who enter employment earlier. Thirdly, as long as public subsidy extends equally throughout the three or four years there is an incentive for students to opt for the longer course. If the balance were shifted, weighting student support (at a more generous level) towards the initial cycle, this would substantially change the pattern of demand. In particular it would favour the participation of groups which are currently under-represented.

Once again the Scottish example is relevant. Young people in Scotland tend to enter higher education earlier than their counterparts elsewhere in the UK. The first year of the Scottish degree is broader, reflecting the breadth of the school curriculum and allowing more choice as to subsequent specialization. There is a choice between the ordinary and the honours degree, though the numbers taking ordinary degrees are declining at present. Thus the structure already exists in embryo for a more radical transformation of the system. It does not mean an amalgamation of the Scottish and English systems, though equivalence will be made easier. The move to a looser temporal framework, with more stages and less adherence to cramping notions of full-time study, would multiply the larger measure of choice which already characterizes the Scottish system.[5]

Issue two: human resources and managing change

Abandoning the gold standard would be a major change. It is a fair bet that the bulk of the resistance would come from inside the system. My second issue is the relationship between innovation, of whatever magnitude, and the staffing of the system. People are the major resource of higher education, more so than almost any other service. How adequate are policies within higher education for developing this resource?

Innovation in higher education suffers from the constraint that its denizens have almost all spent a highly formative part of their youth within it, and have also very largely practised within it throughout their professional lives. In one of his essays on higher education (1985, pp. 58–9), Christopher Ball remarks that people are predisposed to favour the system in which they have been reared (and in which they have almost by definition been relatively successful, at least by the standards of the system); such is the power of habit. Internal impetus for reform is correspondingly hard to achieve. Ideas about what is appropriate as content and structure, and of who is suited to benefit from it, are necessarily shaped by the experience of those who inhabit the system.

This is in no sense to denigrate the potential and the willingness of academics to review their professional practices. Up to a point the same constraint applies to any profession. But it gives a particular character to the type of debate needed to envisage the way forward for higher education. A powerful example is the virtual exclusion of further education from much of the debate. Very few of the participants in the debate (myself included) have not gone the school route to higher education, or have spent time in further education as student or teacher. The structure of the post-secondary system has not made for easy dialogue between the higher and the further sectors. Thus despite the fact that in many respects – student numbers, experience of part-time education, the overall output of the system and the balance between the various grades of technical and non-technical graduates – it seems wrong to exclude FE, endless attention is paid to the division between the university and the polytechnic sector but very little to that between them and the colleges of further education.

The notion of higher education institutions as communities may always have been a myth. We are now witnessing a redivision of labour which exposes and accentuates major differences between categories of academic staff (Schuller 1990). Some of this differentiation is vertical, most noticeably in the polytechnics. Some of it is in the functional changes required of staff at all levels. A multiplicity of skills is required, intellectual, educational and managerial, and this means greater diversity of occupational identity – another plurality to be added to those listed by Ball in Chapter 11. Whilst almost every institution is engaged in burnishing – or creating – its corporate image, far less attention is paid to what membership of the corporation signifies to those employed by it. In spite of significant new initiatives in the way of staff development and appraisal, there is a long way to go. Shattock rightly raises the question of staff loyalty: how will it be divided between the institution and the discipline (see also Becher 1990)? Or will it dissolve entirely?

Governance, it may be argued, is more to do with systems than people. But ultimately it is to do with what Burton Clark in FHE1 called 'the factory floor'. Autonomy, validation and co-ordination, the key themes of FHE1's analysis of governance, all depend on how people approach the tasks in hand. Similarly the maintenance of quality, in teaching, research or administration (and how often that last is missed out in the debate on quality) should arguably be treated not only as a matter of output but of process – a tired term, but one with great implications if taken seriously in relation to higher education. And on access, to take just a simple example, research has shown how far admissions officers can, unconsciously, subvert the stated policy of an institution to broaden its intake (Fulton and Elwood 1989). Reid's chapter shows how essential staff development – and also, incidentally, appropriate recruitment – is if an institution's policy on access is to be implemented. Blackstone's case study confirms the crucial importance of a strategic approach to staffing.

The concluding volume of FHE1, *Excellence in Diversity*, included a section on the academic profession. It bravely tackled the issue of tenure, recommending a shift to employment contracts of the kind common to other parts of the public sector, and went on to propose greater mobility within the system and between higher education and outside organizations. The culture of work within higher education – its pace and timescales – is changing willy-nilly, but arguably without the planning and imagination required.

Is it time to abandon the assumption that academe is a lifetime career? Educationalists – especially in my own area of continuing education – are the first to preach that people need to be flexible, and to be ready to change careers several times in a lifetime. But the structure of the profession makes it difficult for them to do so. The cost – to the institution's effectiveness, and consequently to the students, and also to many academics as individuals – must be considerable though impossible to quantify. Without adequate support, tenure can be a trap as much as a privilege.

But higher education is a particular profession, and I am not arguing for a

dissolution of the lifetime academic career. A single question will do: what is
the best balance to be achieved within the academic profession between
'lifers' and, as it were, recidivists who move in and out of the system? A
learning culture should embrace learning from colleagues with different
backgrounds and experience, as well as the maintenance of traits specific to
the institution or system. Richardson points to the potential contribution
of lay members to academic decision-making, and Perry reminds us that
notions of quality can be enhanced by outside contact. A fresh approach is
needed to recruitment, career development and the organization of academic
work.

For those – still the majority – who commit themselves to academic work
as a lifetime career, we need to review the notion of a career in this context.
There are two particular aspects here. The first is that achievement, potential and responsibility are very loosely, if at all, related. In universities,
academics are promoted for performance in research, with teaching and
administration running a very long way behind. Promotion may mean no
increase or change at all in responsibilities; it is a reward for past achievement. Where it does involve new responsibilities, the link is a curious one, for
the grounds for promotion may say nothing at all about the individual's
ability to perform these new tasks, which are often of a wholly different
character from the work done so far. Talented researchers may make poor
academic managers.

The supposed symbiotic link between teaching and research has been long
debated. Increasingly the link appears valid at a collective rather than an
individual level; in other words there should be cross-fertilization between
teachers and researchers, but any single academic need not combine the two
functions. People get tired of research and of teaching, permanently or
temporarily, and not enough attention is paid to the consequences. Similarly,
the relationship between these recognizable academic activities and that of
'management' needs to be thought through. How far should senior and
middle-ranking personnel be practising academics, or even of academic
origin at all?

The National Health Service has over the past few years seen a significant
change in its management structure and ethos, with the introduction of
general managers at unit, district and regional levels. Some of these have
been drawn from within the ranks of the medical profession, but most have
come from outside. There have been successes and failures, sometimes due to
personalities, sometimes to other factors. On the positive side it is hard to
argue against the need for priorities to be established and matched against
resources, with clear notions of efficiency and responsibility; on the other
side, simplistic notions and techniques derived from private enterprise
cannot be applied to a public service with multiple, often unquantifiable,
objectives.

It is too early to make an overall judgement on the health service initiative, but even at this stage the parallel with higher education is illuminating.
What is the relationship between managers and professionals? Collegiality

may or may not be the hallmark of academic governance, but too much weight on it will cause it to crumble completely. Strict hierarchical management has certainly emerged in many institutions over the last decade as a means of coping with the changing policy context; greater efficiency may have resulted but this is not the same as greater effectiveness, and it remains to be seen what the appropriate structure is in the longer term. Whatever happens, the genie of the notion of 'academic management' is out of the bottle, and it is the *how* not the *whether* which requires debate.

From management to that other filler of airport bookshelves: new technology. There have been many false dawns in the history of educational technology, up to and including the threat of teacherless classrooms throughout schools. Nevertheless the new generation of information technology does seem to offer a particular challenge to the notion of academic activity, especially on the teaching side, as Richardson points out (see also Sargant 1990). It offers access to information at such levels and with such versatility that the notion of the teacher as essentially a repository of higher order knowledge is no longer at all sustainable. Fresh force is given to questions about what constitutes a good teacher and what the appropriate balance is between academic staff in the conventional sense and other 'related' staff such as librarians and technical assistants. There is no reason to suppose that higher education is or should be immune from the questions currently being posed to the schoolteaching profession about the division of labour between professionals and para- or non-professionals, as well as about the qualifications required for entry into the profession. The advent of technology, and the arrival in higher education of cohorts of younger people already accustomed to exploiting it skilfully, will pose serious questions. Will higher education show itself more responsive in this sphere than it has been generally to changes in the school curriculum?

Issue three: continuing education

Thirdly I have selected my own field of continuing education. Although several of FHE1's proposals, such as the introduction of an educational entitlement scheme (Fulton 1981a) or the setting up of local committees to promote the provision of adult and post-experience education (Shattock 1983) directly supported continuing education, it was not the recurrent theme that one might now expect. Much of the agenda here overlaps with the first two issues, so I can be very brief.

Short cycle and part-time higher education are far better suited to the integration of continuing education than the current model. The arguments put forward above concentrated largely on the ability of a foundation degree model to cope with the required expansion, but the shift to a more flexible pattern of shorter cycles would also greatly increase opportunities for adults to return to study at different points. As Williams shows, postgraduate study is already mainly part-time; the model proposed would extend this pattern downwards in two senses. First, it would enable more of those who finished their initial education without a taste of higher education of any kind to return to take a foundation degree. We should not forget the commitment – perhaps gamble is a better term – required of an adult to give up a job and return to a new form of education for a minimum of three years, often extended by a period on an Access course; the shortening of this period should have something of the positive effect on participation referred to by McPherson in relation to the shorter Scottish Higher qualification. Secondly, it would enable those who leave with a foundation degree to return and make this up to an honours degree. This is quite simply the pattern followed by many of those currently doing Masters level work, many of whom have been out at work for substantial periods. This is just as much continuing education as short professional or liberal courses, and there is no reason why the second cycle should not also be seen in that light. The fact that the same stage can be both part of initial education and a tranche of continuing education is a positive benefit.

The implications of a shift of this kind, and of a more general commitment to continuing education on the part of institutions of higher education can be handled only within a broader rethinking of the redivision of academic labour. If there are to be such multiple entry and exit points, that will require sophisticated inter-institutional collaboration and skilful internal management, including staff development. A prominent feature here will be renewed emphasis on the local and regional dimension of higher education. This must be even more the case as part-time education gains in significance, since such students by definition seek access to a network of local institutions (Tight 1991).

It is on quality that perhaps the boldest claim can be made. It is of the essence of the practice of continuing education that it should be educational for the teachers as well as the students. Clichés such as responsiveness and student-centredness come to life when properly applied, with teachers drawing on students' individual and collective experience. Arguably the single best indicator of good practice is whether the educator is learning and developing directly as a result of his or her teaching. In so far as this is further established in continuing than in initial education, the potential effect on quality is enormous – provided only that the lessons can be properly incorporated into the mainstream.

A cluster of further points concern the relation between education and work. The first is to underline the sheer scale of the continuing education task. As Flint points out, 80 per cent of the workforce of the year 2000 is already in employment, and the large majority of these people will have been excluded from further or higher education by the failure to expand earlier. Allied to this is increased longevity, part of the ageing of the population. One of the most significant educational challenges of the coming decade is to meet the needs of the Third Age, in relation to paid and voluntary work as well as leisure time (Schuller and Walker 1990). The combination of demographic and technological change is an immensely powerful one in the demands it places on the education system.

The second point is that the formal education system is not the only player in the game. Dorotea Furth from the OECD referred in the seminar to the emergence of the so-called third sector of post-compulsory education, which in the European context denotes the numerous private agencies who are responding to the demand for continuing education. The challenge to the formal sector is not merely a competitive one; it is to seek ways of complementing private provision in order to provide the optimal range of learning opportunities. Integration into Europe will reinforce the need for mechanisms which allow and encourage mobility between jobs and between educational providers.

Directly related is the notion of educational entitlements as part of good employment practice. Educational institutions obviously have a vested interest in convincing employers of the merits of continuing education; mandatory continuing education, which obliges professionals to participate in regular courses in order to maintain their professional status, offers a guaranteed market. But the idea of entitlement need carry none of this slightly cynical flavour. It means, rather, encouraging a dialogue between institutions, employers and individuals or their trade union representatives in order to secure mutually beneficial development. What would be cynical, however, would be for educational institutions to urge this upon other employers without implementing it in some form themselves. Hypocrisy may be too harsh a term, but universities and colleges do not distinguish themselves as providers of educational opportunities for their own members, especially for non-academic staff. A laissez-faire policy on sabbaticals for academic staff is not adequate. The recurrent theme in this section has been the erosion of boundaries: between full-time and part-time education; between different sectors and different occupational identities; and now finally between educational institutions as providers and as consumers of learning opportunities.

Values, diversity and responsibility: a concluding note

Pervasive though the effect of all the explicit or implicit changes suggested above might be, they skirt round the question of values. Twenty years ago Sir Brian Pippard called for the Free University to make way for the Morally Committed University. This was not a declaration of support for irrational relativism, but for serious attention to be paid to developing what he called creative morality, distinguishing that from 'the academic ideals of detached inquiry which are admirable in the few, but in the many amount to collective irresponsibility.' (Pippard 1972, p. 75). Much more recently the freshly retired President of Harvard University, Derek Bok, placed at the centre of his reflections on Higher Learning the revival of the teaching of ethics as an integral part of all higher education (Bok 1986). It may be time to pick up and transform the goals promoted by the Enterprise in Higher Education initiative, detaching them from any narrow concept of entrepreneurialism and taking seriously the question of responsibility. This would provide a very different resonance to the notion of autonomy so freely used in FHE1 – and perhaps a rallying call for the future.

Unlike FHE1 this reassessment of the future of higher education cannot draw on the authority of a number of distinguished signatories. The authors of subsequent chapters speak for themselves, as I do here. Yet I think it fair to identify two prime conclusions. The first is a simple reassertion of the need for *diversity* in higher education, with the significant addendum that this diversity be extended to include the opportunities offered through the further education sector. The second marks more of a departure from the priorities of the former study, though it is certainly foreshadowed in it. It is best represented by the term *responsibility*. By this I mean two things.

First, institutions, and the system itself, accept the need to make themselves more open, not only in the expected sense of open to students but also in exposing their workings, their achievements and their still to be achieved goals to scrutiny. This scrutiny itself has two components: the external and the internal. The former comprises acceptance of responsibility to account to others for the use of resources – accountability in the literal sense. The latter denotes a specific obligation to promote internal commitment to achieving the diverse range of objectives – scholarship, skills, socialization – that higher education sets itself. This is a corporate responsibility, which cannot be left to individual academics alone. It is the modern version of collegiality.

Secondly, what the institutions produce should be responsible. Again there are two aspects. As creators of knowledge, academics have a responsibility to truth, to the extent that this is available. This must entail the critical function, the challenging of existing tenets and practices. Arguably, one of the most damaging legacies of the last decade has been to downgrade this critical function. But academe can and should be geared to meeting social and economic needs – to acting 'functionally' in that sense – without abandoning its duty to disturb and upset. Students are the other product. Here responsibility equates with empowerment. Equipping students to make choices for themselves, to fashion their own values and to create the means for realizing those values – in short, to take responsibility for themselves – is the task in hand.

I am tempted to a final image. On the one hand is the ski-lift model of education. Students hook themselves onto the T-bar and are tugged upwards as far as they are able to go. Some ride smoothly to the top, and swoop exaltedly amongst the peaks; others dismount, or are shaken off, early on, and mill around on the slushy lower slopes. Once off, they cannot remount. The path of the lift is unidirectional, continous; its users are essentially passive for as long as they are on the bar. On the other hand is the orienteering model. Participants work out their route for themselves, with guidance. They crisscross, up and down, travelling on their own or in teams. They may compete, to world level, or go at their own pace. They choose.

The analogy of course fails, as all analogies do, because the high skiers descend the fastest, ending up at the bottom with the rest. But it may be fit for its purpose, to prime the debate.

Notes

1. One of these is not included here, that on quality by Peter Williams, who helpfully agreed to offer his thoughts as director designate (as he then was) of the CVCP's new Academic Audit Unit but quite understandably was unwilling to commit himself to print so early in office.
2. The Robbins Report spelt out its philosophy in terms of four objectives 'essential to any properly balanced system. We begin with instruction in skills suitable to play a part in the general division of labour ... Secondly ... what is taught should be taught in such a way as to promote the general powers of the mind ... Thirdly, we must name the advancement of learning ... Finally ... the transmission of a common culture and common standards of citizenship.' (Robbins 1963, pp. 6–7; see Tight 1991 p. 120 for a reinterpretation).
3. UNESCO figures for the mid-1980s give an index of this kind; United States and Canada have over 5,000 students per 100,000 inhabitants; all other major industrialized countries between 2,000 and 3,000; the UK has 1795 (quoted in Tight 1991, p. 48).
4. The chapters were submitted before the publication of the White Paper *Higher Education: A New Framework*, which foreshadows a single funding structure for teaching in universities, polytechnics and colleges (DES 1991b, para. 23).
5. The struggle against excessive specialization has a long history in Scotland, magisterially chronicled by George Davie. In doing so he expounds the principle 'found in Adam Smith, Dugald Stewart and the older Scottish writers, that the extension of the division of labour which leads to the material enrichment of the economy also simultaneously leads to its spiritual impoverishment or, in other words, that the intensification of specialization on which the advance of civilization depends tends, by increasingly hindering communication between the persons involved in the various specialized sectors, to dry up the springs of inventiveness in that society.' (Davie 1986, pp. 15–16).

2

Finished and Unfinished Business

Gareth Williams

The SRHE-Leverhulme proposals

The SRHE-Leverhulme Study into the Future of Higher Education (FHE1) was launched in 1979 at a time when, despite policies to encourage participation, age participation rates were lower than they had been a decade earlier. This could be related to the generally stagnant conditions in the graduate labour market during the 1970s; and the study's first report, published in 1981 at a time when the new Conservative government public expenditure cuts were beginning to bite, was not sanguine about graduate job prospects for the next decade (Lindley 1981). There was excess capacity, especially in non-university institutions, and this was reflected in low student–staff ratios and high unit costs. Overseas students' numbers had risen dramatically during the 1970s as universities and polytechnics tried to fill the places that were left empty by the unexpectedly low demand from home students. In 1978 the government had made itself unpopular in universities by trying to impose institutional quotas on the number of students from overseas. In 1978 also, the DES had published its discussion document on *Higher Education into the 1990s* which outlined possible consequences of the decline in the population of school leavers from the mid-1980s onwards and invited reactions from the higher education community about how to deal with it.

But the basic assumptions of the Robbins era were still in place. Expected demand from school leavers 'qualified by ability and attainment' was the mainspring of higher education planning. Everything else, including much of the civil research budget, was linked ultimately to this yardstick. The symbiosis of research and teaching was rarely questioned. Despite fifteen years of the binary policy, the establishment of the Open University, and the wholesale closure of colleges of education (none of which had been envisaged by the Robbins Committee), the essential features of the system were very much what they had been twenty years earlier when the Robbins Report was published. In particular, despite several attempts at drawing new maps of knowledge, the specialized three-year honours degree based on an academic discipline dominated undergraduate studies. Nearly all funds came from central government, via the University Grants Committee (UGC) block grant in the case of the universities and the Advanced Further Education Pool for the non-university institutions.

It was into this atmosphere, which combined stagnation and complacency, that FHE1 was launched. Its basic philosophy, common in the United States but rare on this side of the Atlantic, was one of self-help, the idea that the higher education community could powerfully influence its own future by deciding its aims and objectives and the means of achieving them. Methodologically, the study was based on two basic ideas. First, that a great deal was known in the academic literature about the operation of the higher education system and its relations with the economy and society, but that these academic studies had rarely been disseminated in ways that influenced practical policy making. The second underlying idea was that of networking through the creation of interlocking groups of authors of papers, members of small group seminars, participants in wider conferences and influential individuals from industry and commerce, government and from within higher education. The study produced nine theme reports, each with recommendations. A vital aspect of the dissemination network was the decision by *The Times Higher Education Supplement* to publish a special supplement on each of the main themes. The final publications were a brief report, *Excellence in Diversity* (SRHE-Leverhulme 1983), which pointed a way forward for the 1980s, and a longer monograph, *Response to Adversity* (Williams and Blackstone 1983), which reviewed the themes at rather greater length. They were published during the 1983 election campaign, which may have reduced their immediate public impact, though they were widely reported.

The main aims of the strategy outlined in *Excellence in Diversity* were:

a) to provide opportunities for all who are able to benefit from some form of higher education and to encourage access from a broader social spectrum;
b) to reduce undue specialization in secondary education and the initial years of higher education;
c) to create a climate within which the quality of teaching and research can be maintained, at a time when underlying demographic trends will make competition more difficult;
d) to stimulate research and other academic activities not directly linked to student numbers;
e) to encourage institutions to prepare realistic development plans;
f) to increase the capacity of universities, polytechnics and colleges to respond positively to changing academic, social, economic and industrial needs;
g) to promote efficiency in the use of resources;
h) to create a framework for policy and management studies that will help leaders of academic institutions meet the challenge of adaptation without growth.

Broadly, the report proposed that these aims should be achieved through:

a) diversification so as to provide for the interests and needs of a much wider clientele;
b) the restructuring of basic undergraduate courses so as to provide two years of fairly general initial higher education followed by two years of more specialized study for those who would be going on to specialized professional or academic work;
c) the establishment of a review body to monitor teaching quality in universities;
d) more explicit focusing of research efforts between and within institutions and a clearer separation of funding for teaching and research;
e) radical modification of tenure arrangements in universities;
f) regular performance appraisal of members of academic staff;
g) the erosion but not the abolition of the binary system;
h) more positive policy leadership by central government;
i) diversification of funding sources and mechanisms for both institutions and students;
j) the establishment of a national centre for higher education management and policy studies.

The 1980s

The 1980s was a decade of radical change in British higher education and in several ways it was a period of expansion. Although it started with a 20 per cent public expenditure cut (the removal of any subsidy for overseas students and the 1981 cuts in institutional support, which were the biggest reductions in income ever imposed on British higher education), it ended with student numbers rising rapidly despite continuing financial stringency and the five per cent per year reduction in the number of school leavers. Full-time home student numbers increased from 451,000 in 1979 to 563,000 in 1988. Of this total, 43 per cent were in polytechnics and colleges in 1979 and 52 per cent by 1988. At the same time part-time students grew from 268,000 to 377,000, accounting for 38 per cent of all students enrolled in the later year. Even the number of overseas students was at its highest ever level by the end of the decade (63,000). The total number of students of all kinds rose by 227,000 during the ten year period 1979–1988. This may be compared with a rise of 316,000 during the decade of most rapid expansion from 1962 to 1972. The smallest rise was in full-time student numbers in universities which grew by only four per cent between 1979 and 1987 but by another four per cent in the following year. During the same period the number of students in polytechnics and colleges grew by 50 per cent. The most rapid rate of increase, however, was in part-time postgraduates whose number grew by 64 per cent. Another significant feature of the 1980s was the increased proportion of women students which grew from 42 cent in 1979 to 47 per cent in 1988. Other important changes were the increase in the number of entrants over the age of 21 (from 24 per cent of the total in 1979 to 28 per cent in 1988) and the increase from 410,000 to 571,000 between 1980/81 and 1986/87 in the number of students attending continuing education courses in universities.

In terms of student numbers and the pattern of participation, therefore, the recommendation for a renewal of expansion certainly came about, though whether this was because, or in spite, of government policies is far from clear. In contrast to the 1960s the expansion of student numbers has not been accompanied by a corresponding increase in resources. In universities student–staff ratios increased from 9.3 in 1979/80 to 10.7 in 1987/88. The figures for polytechnics were 8.1 in 1980/81 and 12.9 in 1987/88. Public expenditure per student fell in real terms by about 20 per cent between 1981/82 and 1990/91. In universities the reduction was less than ten per cent while in non-university institutions it was over 25 per cent.

Not surprisingly, the final report did not recommend cuts in higher education expenditure but it did recognize that 'expenditure has to be restrained in an activity that must remain largely in the public sector' (p. 2). Apart from this, many of the recommendations with respect to mechanisms and forms funding have been put into effect, at least partly. A mixed system of student grants and loans was advocated in two of the interim reports and the final report concluded that 'provided repayment arrangements are geared to realistic assessments of ability to pay, student support through loans is at least as equitable as support through means tested grants' (p. 12). It would be fair to conclude that the authors had in mind a system in which repayment would be more closely linked to subsequent earnings than the scheme actually introduced by the government.

The report foresaw the explicit division of institutional income into five categories: core income from central government; fees; and full-cost funding of contract research and teaching by central government, local authorities and employers. At the beginning of the 1980s the universities received two-thirds of their funds in the form of an undifferentiated block grant from the UGC. It was suggested that this figure might fall to about 50 per cent. In fact as we begin the 1990s the share provided by the Universities Funding Council (UFC) will fall well below 50 per cent and is divided explicitly into research and teaching components. The teaching component is related explicitly to student numbers, fees are to rise to about 20 per cent of the total and there have been substantial increases in income earned from services rendered. With the exceptions of the research component (for which non-university institutions have never received any general funding) and the major reform of the 1988 Education Reform Act which gave polytechnics and many colleges their financial independence, the changes in the non-university sector have been broadly similar.

British higher education institutions are now operating largely as market-oriented service enterprises. One problem, as Williams and Blackstone (op. cit.) pointed out, is that the information feedback mechanisms which are essential for successful markets operate in higher education only with considerable lags and uncertainty. However, subject to certain safeguards to protect quality and equity, the report supported the idea of channelling a considerably larger amount of financial support through students rather than directly to institutions and the provision of funds through a multiplicity of mechanisms rather than single block grants. The main safeguard required was the establishment of reliable quality assurance mechanisms. Amongst proposals for the improvement of quality were the formal appraisal of academic staff on a regular basis, the modification of lifetime tenure as the principal form of employment contract for university teachers and the establishment by the universities of a collective quality assurance agency. It would be presumptuous to claim that FHE1 was the only source of these innovations but they can certainly be included in any list of recommendations that have been implemented.

Williams and Blackstone thought that a variety of funding sources would be likely to be to the long run advantage of higher education both quantitatively and qualitatively. It is too early to say whether this claim has been borne out. However, there is no doubt that the higher education of the 1990s is much more consumer oriented than that of the 1970s. There have been very substantial increases in the amount of institutional income earned from the sale of teaching, research and other services and pricing policies for these commercial activities are based on much more realistic estimates of real costs. (See Williams 1992 and Williams and Loder 1991.)

The changes in higher education funding that occurred during the 1980s do, however, raise fundamental questions about the character of universities and polytechnics as academic institutions, irrespective of the latest White Paper's proposed removal of the binary line (DES 1991b). One 'idea of the university' is that its only proper function is to teach undergraduate and postgraduate students and to undertake basic research. Any other activity is a distraction and is justified only if it generates a surplus which can be used to advance teaching and research.

At the other extreme is the view that universities and polytechnics are economic enterprises in the knowledge industry, and it is appropriate for them to sell whatever mix of academic services is most cost-effective to produce. Before 1981, selling conventional undergraduate and postgraduate courses paid for out of public funds was indisputably the most profitable activity and issues about whether or not it was appropriate to undertake other work were of marginal significance. When universities used some of their resources to undertake public service activities, these were usually deemed both marginal and complementary to the central academic activities of the institution.

If core public funding is insufficient to maintain its existing size and organizational structure, a university or polytechnic has the choice either of contracting until it is viable within its core resources, or of expanding its income from other sources. The question arises of whether the academic integrity of the university or polytechnic is best maintained by keeping staff together even if they spend a substantial part of their time on activities that are not strictly academic, or whether the 'idea' of the university as a haven of disinterested scholarship is more important than the individuals who constitute any actual university. The second position would imply that staff should be shed in order for the university to be able to confine itself to its proper functions of education and basic research. Nearly everybody both inside and outside the universities in practice accepts the former, more pragmatic, position but its implications for the nature of higher education have yet to be fully analysed.

Market forces are not necessarily damaging. One of the strengths of the European university is its capacity to adapt to changing circumstances. However, it is important to be aware that fundamental change is taking place and that it may have very profound consequences for the nature of academic institutions.

Henry Wasser, writing from the perspective of the United States and several continental European countries, where similar changes in higher education funding are taking place, is in no doubt that a sea change is occurring:

> Obviously the university as a long-lived institution has survived by constantly adjusting to changing social and political needs. Yet the present rapid and radical move to a university adaptive in a major fashion to economic development, to an entrepreneurial university, would appear to go beyond modification to a sufficiently changed structure that no longer for many institutions fits the time-honored definition of a university. (Wasser 1990, pp. 110–22)

An alternative view is that just as universities in the nineteenth and early twentieth century adapted to the needs of a meritocratized Civil Service and liberal professions, so the higher education of the late twentieth century is adapting to the need to promote, and to prepare people for, the high technology, information-rich society and market-driven economies of the twenty-first century.

In the polytechnics substantial management changes accompanied the transformation to corporate status in April 1989. It is too early to evaluate the effects of these changes on the academic ethos of these institutions but there can be no doubt that financial exigencies brought them about. Management changes under way include tighter line management, more rigorous definition of the terms of academic staff contracts and the establishment of polytechnic companies to sell consultancy services. There have been similar management changes in the universities but in general they have been more evolutionary and incremental. As a result there has been considerable change during the 1980s in most universities and, since 1989, in the polytechnics in the speed at which they can respond to external opportunities.

An agenda for the 1990s

FHE1 aimed to identify 'major issues that should be on the policy agenda during the next fifteen years whatever the nature of the governments, agencies and institutions that formulate and implement the detailed policies.' We are now more than halfway through that fifteen-year period and this paper has shown that the reports have proved to have a record of diagnosis and prediction that is well above average in social forecasting. However, much remains to be done and new tasks have appeared.

Specialization and the structure of degree courses

The evidence on whether there has yet been fundamental change in qualitative and structural features of higher education is inconclusive. Basic course structures have changed relatively little. In 1979 66 per cent of students below postgraduate level were on degree courses and in 1988 the figure was 65 per cent. Amongst full-time students the proportion on degree courses remained at 82 per cent throughout the decade. Apart from a very slight fall in the proportions of students in medicine and the humanities the pattern of students by broad subject group has remained almost stable throughout the decade of the 1980s. These figures include both universities and non-university institutions.

The specialized three-year honours degree remains dominant in England and Wales and its four-year equivalent has, as a result of financial stringency, actually increased in importance in Scotland. When they were asked by the UGC in 1984 universities were almost unanimous in rejecting the recommendation for broader two-year initial courses, and they have shown little enthusiasm for fundamental change since then, though there have been several incremental changes resulting mainly from financial pressures. The Higginson proposals for the radical reform of the A level examination to reduce specialization was rejected out of hand by the government (see for example, Higginson 1990). The net result of this obduracy by both universities and government is that excessive and premature specialization remains, as it was at the time of Robbins, the curse of English secondary and higher education. On the positive side there has been the introduction of the AS level as a subsidiary higher education entry qualification and there are signs that at least some subjects in some universities are beginning to accept it as a legitimate indicator of ability to pursue degree courses. Innovations such as the Enterprise in Higher Education Initiative of the Training Agency which are intended to encourage a broadening of the undergraduate curriculum are beginning to scratch the surface of the problem but it is doubtful if they are doing much more.

The most important piece of unfinished business is in this area of course structure and content. Like most commentators on English higher education the authors of the final report disapproved of what they saw as excessive specialization which was having a serious backwash effect in the schools right back to before GCE O level examinations. One of the main recommendations was that 'a wide ranging debate is needed about the content of undergraduate courses in the light of contemporary needs' (p. 6). The report took the bold step of naming the specialized three-year honours degree rather than the A level examination as the main villain of the piece. It quoted Lord Robbins himself in support of the claim that the expansion of specialized degree courses in the 1960s and 1970s was not intended by the Committee (Robbins 1980).

What *Excellence in Diversity* recommended was the replacement of the existing pattern of three-year honours degrees followed by a one-year Masters and a two- or three-year PhD (3+1+2/3), with a 2+(1+1)+2 system. The first two years would lead to a pass degree which might be followed by a further year leading to an honours degree or two years leading to a Masters. Subsequently successful completion of a further two years' full-time study would lead to a research or professional doctorate.

The report claimed that:

> shorter initial courses accompanied by genuine possibilities of credit transfer between institutions and a variety of subsequent options would permit greater flexibility and give individual students more opportunity to tailor their higher education to meet their own particular needs and interests ... a two-year pass degree could be the link which brings together several ideas currently under discussion for shorter, less specialized, more flexible, more widely available basic courses. (SRHE-Leverhulme 1983, p. 8)

It recognized that:

> a two-year pass degree would require radical rethinking of both undergraduate curricula and the pattern of postgraduate studies. A student obtaining a Pass degree would need to have ... a credential that had some intrinsic value and was recognized by both employers and by those who control entry to subsequent specialized courses. (ibid., p. 10)

This central proposal of the strategy was explicitly rejected by universities in 1984 when the idea was put to them by the UGC. Polytechnics and colleges, consulted by the National Advisory Board (NAB), showed more interest but were unwilling to act except jointly with the universities. Subsequently the idea was buried in the deluge of other radical changes that confronted higher education during the rest of the 1980s.

One widespread change on which there is regrettably little quantitative global evidence is the modularization of courses and the development of intra-institutional and inter-institutional credit transfer schemes that enable students to select their own routes through degree and other courses on a reasonably flexible basis. However, these credit transfer schemes have grown up on an *ad hoc* basis and very few of them permit students to obtain an interim qualification that has any currency except as a stage in building up enough credits to qualify for an honours degree – the Open University being a very important exception. This puts a new perspective on the two-year degree proposal in that the alternative is no longer a well structured system of three-year honours degrees but a rather chaotic development of local credit transfer arrangements.

The under-resourced expansion of the 1980s, the introduction of student loans, the increased diversity of the higher education system and the prospects of closer links with our European partners also combine to make a serious review of course structures even more necessary in the 1990s than it was in the previous decade. It is no longer true that all higher education in all subject areas is, or needs to be, packaged into discrete units of three years' duration. In some subjects longer periods of study are necessary to reach a level at which professional practice is possible: this already happens in medicine and a few engineering courses. In many others a shorter period would permit the acquisition of worthwhile knowledge and skills. The real question is what recognition ought to be given to those who succeed in accumulating fewer modules than are currently needed to qualify for an honours degree. This is a particularly important consideration if the British move to mass higher education is to avoid the weaknesses in many European systems of mass entry but also mass drop-out without credit, because full degree qualifications are not obtained. In the United States students in many institutions are able to leave with some appropriate accreditation from almost any stage of their courses and these credits are encashable both in the labour market and as a qualification for further study.

It is a pity that public discussion of the proposals on course structures concentrated on the initial two-year building block and did not recognize that this was put forward in the context of the need for a radical review of all undergraduate and postgraduate courses. The UGC was disingenuous in its 1984 enquiry when it asked universities whether they would support two-year degrees without any recognition of the implications for subsequent study. An alternative way of presenting the proposal would be to stress the need for four-year courses, at least in some subject areas, to enable students to reach adequate breadth and professional specialization, but with the option of a break at the end of two years for those who were more interested in a basic experience of higher education without subsequent specialization. The political debate on student loans in the late 1980s also ignored the point made in the Report that grants for two years followed by partial loans for subsequent study would both encourage access and help to limit the amount of public expenditure devoted to student support. This effect would be strengthened if some of the two-year courses were designed to be able to be delivered at local further education colleges enabling more students to live at home before transferring to a more distant polytechnic or university for higher level studies.

Any serious study of the structure of academic study in the 1990s must include postgraduate qualifications. Postgraduate study is usually neglected in any consideration of higher education policy. It was virtually ignored by Robbins and FHE1 had little to say on the matter. Yet there are now nearly 140,000 postgraduate students, 14 per cent of all students and more than the total number of university students at the time of Robbins. As already mentioned, part-time postgraduate student numbers have been growing particularly rapidly. Any reform of undergraduate studies along the lines suggested in this chapter would inevitably have major implications for post-graduate study. There are increasing doubts about the economic value of many research degrees. There have also been many criticisms of the academic value of the traditional very narrowly focused academic thesis leading to a rigidly discipline-based PhD as the single pinnacle of the educational system. However, the present haphazard growth of master's degrees and diploma courses in response primarily to anticipated niches in the market also has its dangers.

Many of the claims about the symbiotic relationship between research and teaching, which are now widely rejected, remain true for much postgraduate study. As research and teaching are further separated the effects on post-graduate study will be considerable. Should institutions that are not in the first rank of research have the right to offer what purports to be research training? Should they have the right to offer equally prestigious qualifications that are professionally based? This is an area that is almost certain to be of much more policy interest in the 1990s than it has been up to now.

The honours degree based on three or four years of full-time study was established at a time when students came from a few schools and the great majority of graduates made their careers in a narrow range of liberal professions. It has shown itself to be remarkably durable, but it has been enormously helped by the fact that students on full-time degree courses have received mandatory grants, while part-timers and those on other courses have, at best, been eligible for lower value discretionary grants.

Students have a wide range of interests. Some want knowledge and skills that can be obtained only in a three-year honours degree but, given the chance, many would prefer to organize their higher education differently. Over a third of today's students are part-time and their number would increase considerably if part-time students had access to the same financial support as full-timers. Many would come from groups under-represented in the current system. A key issue for higher education in the 1990s is the need for even greater diversity of courses. Increasing 'access' to higher education, whether for equity reasons or to provide the qualified people necessary to improve Britain's economic performance, requires a reappraisal of the content and structure of degree courses. We do not have to envisage education as a commodity and potential students as supermarket shoppers. But we do need to think about whether what is offered is appropriate for the varied needs of a wide clientele.

One advantage of the scheme being proposed here is that it would enable more students to have higher education at less cost to the public purse. If grants from public funds were available only for foundation courses, 50 per cent more students could receive financial support at the same cost to the Exchequer. In practice, many students would continue with third and fourth years. However, many would do specialized courses linked to particular occupations and would be well placed to take loans or to obtain employer sponsorship. Thus a shift of financial support towards foundation courses and part-time modes of study would go a long way towards resolving the central dilemma of higher education policy in the 1990s – how to increase participation to the levels of our economic competitors at a cost that is bearable to taxpayers.

It is no part of this agenda to dilute the internationally recognized high quality of the best of British higher education. To those who consider any proposal to change as signs of a willingness to sacrifice quality for quantity there are three responses. First, British higher education is a classic case of the best being the enemy of the good. In our efforts to preserve all the features of a Rolls Royce higher education we have neglected the virtues of the Ford Fiesta. Second, it is not 'quality' but 'qualities' that we should be considering. Higher education serves a wide variety of purposes and high quality in one context may be merely inefficiency in another. Third, the provision of mass higher education based on two-year foundation degrees would enable the traditional excellence of honours degrees to be concentrated on specialist postgraduate courses that would need to follow them. Reform of postgraduate education would be an important secondary consequence of these proposals. Higher education is one of the few areas of activity in which Britain is still recognized as an international leader. But the world does not stand still. The decline of much of our manufacturing industry since the days when 'Made in Britain' was a guarantee of quality shows the dangers of being content to rest on our laurels.

Quality and content

FHE1 clearly foresaw that diversification and moves towards market funding would put the quality of higher education under pressure. One example of this occurred when overseas student fees were raised and there was evidence that sometimes corners were cut in order to increase overseas recruitment. Concern about quality in the 1990s is likely to continue and to be more generalized. There will continue to be a collective interest in quality assurance mechanisms of the trade association type to ensure adherence to minimum quality thresholds, and some institutions at least will try to sell some of their services on a quality premium basis. Given the nature of higher education it will be even more important than in markets generally, but also even more difficult to ensure, that claims about quality premiums are justified.

Competition for students and the cash they bring with them will encourage institutions to produce hyped-up and sometimes misleading publicity and prospectuses. Funds for innovations in teaching seem likely to be particularly at risk, as bidding systems and reliance on less than full-cost fees encourage marginal cost-pricing, which will inevitably favour expansion of existing courses rather than the development of new ones. There may be similar effects in research if competitive bidding for research projects becomes more prevalent. The need to generate income will encourage an emphasis on short-term money earning activities at the expense of those whose return is less tangible or longer term.

Conversely, however, a market environment will also underline the advantages of a total quality ethos in which all aspects of the work of a university, polytechnic or college are focused on producing services that are attractive to customers. Quality competition is as much a feature of markets as price-cutting. The problem with quality management in higher education will remain that identified in FHE1. In marketing terms higher education institutions are essentially multi-product enterprises in which the value of much of the output is intangible and not able to be easily identified, especially in the short run. It cannot readily be translated into monetary terms.

A *higher education think-tank*

The other main recommendation where little progress has been made is the establishment of a national centre for higher education policy studies. It is an idea that has commended itself to several individuals and groups and a number of proposals were made during the decade to establish such a group, including the establishment of a joint CVCP-CDP working party. However, up to the present little progress has been made for two main reasons. One is that no one has been able to raise the necessary cash; but more fundamentally there has been little agreement about what the principal mission of the centre would be. One school of thought appears to want what would be primarily a sophisticated lobby for higher education that would provide reliable information for resource bargaining with government. Another thinks in terms of a staff college for senior management of universities, polytechnics and colleges.

Despite the lack of agreement this recommendation also is even more relevant in the 1990s than it was in the 1980s. The much greater degree of independence of higher education institutions, their financial autonomy and their competitive environment increases the need for an independent centre. It is important, however, that the centre should be as much critical observer of higher education institutions, even if sympathetic, as advocate on their behalf. An interesting difference between Britain and the United States in the literature on higher education policy is that in Britain the arguments are usually directed towards the government, while in the United States most studies are addressed to the higher education institutions themselves in the belief that as autonomous institutions their future is in their own hands. As our system comes to resemble that of the United States in other ways it is important that the focus of policy discussions on higher education should shift also. Obviously a major task of any independent higher education policy centre would be to subject any public policy initiatives and government claims about its performance to rigorous analysis, but if it were seen merely as a front for any particular interest group, or even as an uncritical advocate of higher education in general it would lose much of its potential value. Thus a national centre with some core funding, preferably from a research council or a charitable trust needs also to be free to seek funding from a wide variety of sources for its research and analysis.

Concluding comments

The pattern of development in higher education is, of course, affected by the general economic and political situation, in particular the results of general elections. No one can pretend that the development of British higher education during the 1980s was uninfluenced by the fact that throughout the period there was a secure government with powerful right-wing radical convictions; nor that, if there were a change of government in the 1990s, higher education would be unaffected. However, the theme of this paper is that much of what happened during the 1980s was predictable and that FHE1 did predict it. Evidence that changes were not simply the result of British government policy is provided by a recent OECD report on changing patterns of finance in higher education (Williams 1990). That report shows that in nearly all OECD countries, there is discussion of, and experimentation with, new and alternative funding mechanisms and forms of institutional management. Changes in institutional funding which are either under way or being discussed in several countries include increased sophistication of the formulae used in determining the allocations to each institution, greater financial autonomy for the institutions, increased proportion of income from student fees and a larger share of income coming from contracts with commercial organizations. In general, there has been a growing interest by many governments in the introduction of an element of market types of organization and incentives in all their higher education institutions.

It is unlikely that any European country will go as far in this direction as the United States, but it is equally unlikely that any foreseeable British government will rapidly reverse trend. The maintenance of high quality in the face of expanding student numbers, rapidly changing technology and inadequate public funding will remain the principal challenge facing higher education during the 1990s.

3

Widening the Access Argument

Andrew McPherson

Introduction

The FHE1 blueprint was intended to increase and widen access to higher education and to change its form, principally by finding a new 'balance' between 'the producer-dominated, the bureaucrat-dominated, and the consumer-dominated models of higher education provision' (Williams 1983, p. 241; also Williams and Blackstone 1983). Increased access meant the admission to higher education of larger numbers of students and larger proportions of the groups from which they came. Wider access meant a greater proportionate increase in the admission of students from under-represented groups than of students from other groups. The proposals on access were linked to the proposals on forms of provision. Wider access and changes in form were advocated both for their own sake and as a means to increase access.

The arguments on access were also shaped by three more specific considerations. One was demographic decline, the correctly anticipated fall in the number of eighteen-year-olds between 1983 and 1995. Another was the sluggish Age Participation Rate (APR) of the 1970s. The APR was an official statistic that expressed the number of 'young' entrants (i.e. aged under 21 years) to higher education anywhere in the United Kingdom as a percentage of a base population of eighteen-year-olds one year previously. In 1979/80, the British APR stood at 12.4 which was lower than it had been, at 13.8, in 1970/71 (DES 1990a; Farrant 1981, Table 2.4). This led FHE1 to doubt that the traditional English system (of school leavers with two or more GCE A levels taking full-time three-year honours degrees) could sustain a sufficient increase in rates of participation in higher education to compensate numerically for the coming demographic decline. The third factor was the political climate and, in particular, the letter to the universities from the University Grants Committee (UGC) in July 1981.The letter led to cuts in university places. It further marginalized the Robbins principle of access for all those qualified and willing (CHE 1963, para. 31) and it foreshadowed greater central government intervention in higher education affairs. In consequence, this was how FHE1 saw the overall problem in the early 1980s:

> Higher education institutions as a whole face, therefore, the challenge of adaptation without growth. They will either have change forced upon them as large-scale excess capacity begins to emerge, or they will adapt in an attempt to attract new types of client.
>
> It is against this Hobson's choice that we make our proposals for a radical reform of British higher education. (Williams and Blackstone 1983, p. 36)

In the event, this has not quite been the choice. The British Age Participation Index (API) (a measure virtually identical for present purposes to the former APR – see above) rose more or less continuously in the 1980s, from 12.7 in 1980/81 to 15.2 in 1988 (DES 1990a). This increase was accompanied by a small increase after 1982 in the proportion of home full-time new entrants to higher education who were aged 21 or over. The net result was that, despite demographic decline, the numbers of home full-time new entrants to higher education rose modestly in the middle 1980s, and more substantially towards the end of the decade (DES 1988a; DES 1990b, Table 3).

This rise in student numbers and in rates of participation has attenuated what FHE1 had thought might become a major institutional (college and university) motive for change. At the same time, however, a potentially more fundamental basis for change has emerged with the impending introduction of a market in students. With a rise in the proportion of institutional income derived from student fees, all institutions of higher education will have a direct and continuing financial interest in the numbers of students they can attract. Nevertheless, the implications for access are far from clear. Government now agrees that access must increase, and accepts the FHE1 view that non-traditional approaches are paramount. But it is more concerned with increased access than with wider access, except as a necessary means to the former (DES 1987), and its policy for student loans has conflicting implications both for increasing and for widening the entry to higher education.

The argument of this chapter is as follows. The social basis of student demand for higher education is more buoyant than earlier assumed, and traditional secondary education more effective. Non-traditional developments in access, though vigorous, remain marginal to mainstream higher education. They risk further marginalization as numbers on traditional routes grow, especially after 1995. Though the argument for increased access may have been won after a fashion, the argument for wider access has not. Adequately to fulfil either objective requires an integration of traditional and non-traditional provision. This will not be easy in an expanding and differentiated system of higher education permeated by markets. One distinct possibility is that tertiary education will recapitulate the history of secondary schooling this century by replacing inequalities of access to an elite and relatively undifferentiated form of higher education defined by level, with inequalities of access within a more universal, but also more differentiated, form of higher education defined by stage. Whether this matters is partly a question of whether one deprecates unfairness and the loss of talent that accompanies unfairness. But steep inequalities at a high overall level of access are arguably preferable to comparably steep inequalities at a low overall level.

The rest of this chapter amplifies these arguments.

The social basis of student demand

FHE1 assumed that student numbers could be maintained during the fifteen years of demographic decline only if higher education itself changed in ways that might attract more students:

> the present structure and organization has reached its limit: if participation is to be increased, higher education will have to change. (Fulton 1981a, p. 13)

However, the social basis of higher education demand is more buoyant than previously assumed. The authors of FHE1 were aware that the demographic decline was concentrated in the Registrar General's social classes III, IV and V (Farrant 1981, p. 61). Because these groups made only a minority contribution, numerically and proportionately, to student numbers, it was rightly assumed that any fall in new student entrants would be proportionately less than the fall in the number of eighteen-year-olds. It was also thought that the gradual shift in the occupational structure from manual to non-manual employment would have similar implications (DES 1984).

What was not appreciated at the time, however, was that young people's demand for higher education would rise as a result of the rising level of parental education. The higher the level of parental education, the higher tends to be the attainment of the child. It is not just a matter of graduate parents wanting graduate offspring (Rudd 1987; Redpath and Harvey 1987), or that the children of graduate parents are more likely to 'qualify' for higher education with two or more A level passes (Jesson and Gray 1990). The crucial points are that any level of parental education above the minimum tends to boost filial chances of qualifying for higher education; and that this effect has remained constant over a decade in which the proportion of parents with post-compulsory schooling has steadily increased (Burnhill *et al.* 1990). The rate of increase in the proportion of eighteen-year-olds having parents with more than a minimum level of schooling is likely to be steeper in the 1990s than it was in the 1980s. This will tend to boost the proportions qualifying for higher education with two or more A levels or with three or more SCE Highers, even if traditional patterns of school certification remain unreformed. The likelihood, too, is that the increasing proportion of graduates in the parental population will have an additional effect on demand. These changes in the social composition of the school population will also tend to boost mature demand if, as seems likely, 'mature students of the present type ... follow demographic trends similar to the eighteen-year-old population' (Williams and Blackstone 1983, p. 36), and especially if the pre-tertiary system, of schooling and of non-advanced further education (NAFE), remains sub-optimal.

The effectiveness of the traditional route

There is widespread and longstanding agreement that it is the A level that constitutes the main barrier to participation in higher education for young and mature alike in England and Wales (Duffy 1990; Higginson 1990). But FHE1 thought it unrealistic to hope for change in the English and Welsh sixth form (Williams 1983, p. 243), and this was confirmed, at least for the life of Mrs Thatcher's administration, when the government rejected the Higginson committee proposals for broadening the A level curriculum (DES 1988b).

Even the A level, however, is not so bad that it wholly stifled growth in demand in the 1980s when, as we have seen, the API rose. One reason for this was the improvement in young persons' qualifications. The Qualified Leaver Index (QLI) is an official statistic that expresses the percentage of leavers from schools or from courses in NAFE who 'qualify' for entry to higher education by attaining or surpassing the conventional threshold of two GCE A level passes or three SCE Higher grade passes. Between 1979/80 and 1988/89, the British QLI rose from 14.7 to 17.2 (DES 1990a). It is likely, therefore, that social and demographic change in the 1990s will produce higher proportions of school leavers qualifying for higher education despite a sub-optimal pre-tertiary system. Reform of that system would provide a further boost, but the prospects for such reform are uncertain.

How much more could the traditional route to higher education achieve? The example of Northern Ireland provides one indication. In 1987/88, 22 per cent of school leavers in Northern Ireland qualified for higher education by passing two or more A levels (CSO 1990, Table 9.9). Comparable figures for eighteen-year-old leavers from NAFE in Northern Ireland are not available, so a comparison with England and Wales based on the QLI cannot be made. The question can, however, be answered from Scotland which supplies a realistic lower estimate of the potential of traditional schooling to boost higher education demand. In 1987/88 the Scottish QLI was 22.5 (SED 1990a, Table 1). A separate QLI for England and Wales is not published, but the British QLI (including Scotland) in the following year was only 17.2 (DES 1990a). The higher Scottish QLI is paralleled by a higher API. In 1988/89, the Scottish API was 21.2 (SED 1990b, Table 15) compared with a British API (including Scotland) of 15.2 (DES 1990a). In June 1990, the Scottish API was projected to rise to 30.7 per cent by the year 2000 (SED 1990a).

FHE1 did not itself set targets for participation, but the Scottish figures can be compared with four targets proposed in recent years:

1. a British API of 20 per cent by 2000 (DES 1987, para. 2.7);
2. a 50 per cent increase in student numbers (mostly part-time) by the year 2000 (Ball 1990, p. 4);
3. a doubling of student numbers in the next 25 years (Baker 1989);
4. a British API of 24 per cent by 2000 (MacGregor 1990).

Scotland surpassed target 1 in 1987/88. Put in terms of full-time young entrants, target 2 would imply a British API of around 22 to 24 per cent by 2000. Scotland is already close to achieving this. Its projected API of 31 per cent in 2000 represents a doubling of the British API in 1988/89, but in under half the time envisaged by target 3. It is projected that Scotland will reach target 4 in 1990/91 (SED 1990a).

What is more, all these Scottish figures, including the projections, are underestimates of the potential demand for higher education that a traditional system can produce. Ball (1990, p. 3) has talked of the 'vicious circle' whereby low aspirations for education in the general population reinforce low standards of provision which, in turn, keep aspirations low; and he concludes that:

> the main impediment to growth is not lack of student demand for places, but shortage of places for those who apply and could benefit. (ibid. para. 8.2)

The Scottish and British APIs in the 1980s, and the projections of demand to which the APIs lead, are all depressed by the shortage of places in the early and middle 1980s for those who had qualified. One indicator of this is the Qualified Participation Index (QPI). The QPI is the number of young entrants (aged under 21 years) to full-time higher education in the UK expressed as a percentage of school or NAFE college leavers from the previous session. The British QPI fell sharply in the early 1980s following the cuts in university places, and it regained its 1981/82 level only in 1988/89 (DES 1990a). But the Scottish QPI in 1988/89 had still not regained its level of the early 1980s. As Paterson (forthcoming) has demonstrated, one reason for this is that school leavers' propensities to apply to higher education are influenced by their perception of their chances of success. Paterson studied applications to university among Scottish school leavers over the period 1970–1988. He found that aggregate contraction of university places in the early 1980s was associated with a fall in an individual's chances of applying to university, even after the analysis had taken account of gender and social background and of changing levels and patterns of school qualifications. In other words, levels of provision influence levels of student demand.

The marginality of non-traditional access

Non-traditional routes to higher education have diversified and expanded since 1983 (Fulton 1989; Leiven 1989). But initial higher education remains a predominantly full-time activity (though this is partly a matter of how one counts part-timers), predominantly for the young (DES 1990b, Tables 3 and 4). Some higher education institutions have changed and adapted, but a recent survey of 25 universities and colleges found that neither national policy nor shortfalls in particular subject areas were leading to drastic change in admissions or provision (Fulton and Ellwood 1989; pp. 4 and 5; also Fulton 1989). Significantly, most of these institutions were optimistic about their future student numbers.

To make non-traditional access more central to the concerns of institutions, FHE1 proposed that 25 per cent of higher education places be reserved for non-traditional admission. One effect of such quotas could be to encourage changed patterns of provision and, indirectly therefore, to make institutions more accessible to all types of student. There are, nevertheless, several arguments against quotas. First, in an unexpanded system of higher education, changes in the composition of the student body can have only small effects on the chances of entry of disadvantaged groups; and the effect on between-group relativities in the chances of entry are even smaller. Second, wider access for whom? Gender, generation and social class are orthogonal dimensions of inequality, and so, too, in some degree, are ethnicity and region. Where higher education is rationed, the reduction of inequality in one dimension is at the expense of any reduction in another. Which do we choose? Third, unless they lead to changed forms of provision, quotas can solve neither the problem of increased access, nor that of wider access. Quotas exclude as well as include, and are not easily reconciled with a policy for greater student numbers. Moreover, quotas would raise the 'going rate' of qualifications required of entrants by traditional routes. But a higher proportion of disadvantaged than of advantaged applicants for higher education tends to cluster around the threshold of the going qualifications rate. The application of quotas would raise that rate and thereby tend to exclude the very types of students they were designed to admit. Finally, advocates of quotas sometimes argue that traditional school examinations are a poor guide to the potential for success in higher education. This is a tenable position in respect of systems or periods in which access to traditional qualifications is restricted. In such circumstances, an individual's lack of qualifications tells one little about his or her potential for higher education. But it does not follow that the possession of school qualifications is also a poor guide to higher-education potential, still less that conventional qualifications are a worse guide than non-traditional indicators.

The problems raised by quotas are but one instance of the pressing need to reconcile traditional forms of access and provision with the non-traditional.

Markets and higher education for all

It is difficult to anticipate the effect on access of the market in students. The operation of the market will be affected by various interventions including performance indicators, price-fixing and subsidies to institutions and individuals. But the effect of these interventions is mainly a matter of political choice as, too, is the effect of student loans. In general, a market in students will ensure that student numbers become a central consideration for all universities and colleges. But there will also be more specific effects. One feature of markets is that producers influence demand. Access thus becomes a question, not so much about how institutions select, but about how they actively recruit and about the product they offer. This product is itself likely to become more differentiated, with a greater range of types and levels of course on offer. Markets dislike status impediments to participation in them: the suppliers of higher education should be free to supply, and the consumers should be free to consume, when, where, what and how they wish. So the differentiation that accompanies the advent of a market makes standards, or quality assurance, a central issue. It is in the name of standards that we charter providers to provide and consumers to consume. Without a currency of standards, there could be no market, no outcomes of higher education, no purpose to the whole enterprise. Yet standards also restrict the operation of the market. Institutions may be reluctant to see charters extended to other institutions. An individual's qualifications at one stage may also constitute a restriction on progression to the next.

These features of markets – the emphasis on the supply side, the greater product range, and the intolerance of impediments to participation – are likely to accelerate a change that was happening in and around FHE1, a change which had its origins, not in the move towards markets, but in an older tradition of non-formal provision. This a change in the definition of higher education itself.

The FHE1 proposal was for a system with multiple entry-points, and these are developing with credit accumulation and transfer, exemptions, franchising, wider-access schemes and the accreditation of prior experiential learning (Parry and Wake 1990). There was also a proposal to replace the three-year honours degree with a two-year degree, for which students would be grant supported, followed by various loan-supported postgraduate courses (Williams and Blackstone 1983). Essentially the FHE1 strategy was to make higher education more accessible by making it more general and therefore easier, shorter and cheaper (though one might question whether general education is necessarily easier). At least for the initial cycle of higher education, the plan envisaged a single, common exit point and exit standard. More meant different, but not that different.

Since then, the argument has moved on. Why stop at multiplying entry routes? Why not multiple modes of participation (part-time, franchised, accredited, punctuated, distance) and also multiple exit points? This line of thought brings together a number of concerns in the access argument, namely: the interfaces between school, NAFE and higher education; the relationship of higher education with continuing education; the control of quality by means of the control of exit criteria, rather than criteria relating to entry or participation; and the variety and responsiveness of higher education institutions themselves. In principle, a model with multiple modes of entry, participation and exit opens the way to universal higher education. It does this partly by the economies of provision that are made possible by the recognition of equivalences (between, say, formal learning and learning from experience), but principally by detaching the concept of higher education from the gold standard of a completed degree (whether two, three or four years).

An important move in this direction came in 1984 with the reformulation by the UGC and the National Advisory Board of the Robbins access principle. The new principle, accepted by government in 1985, was that:

> courses of higher education should be available for all those who are able to benefit from them and who wish to do so. (DES 1985, para. 3.2)

Thus the 'ability to benefit' from whatever a higher education institution offers becomes the criterion for participation, not the ability to excel in, or even to complete, a higher-education course. In principle, with sufficient modes of participation and sufficient entry and exit points, all can take part. In such a model, one can enter at any point and leave at any point and, provided one has grown in between, one has had access to higher education. Like secondary education before it, higher education ceases to be a level and becomes a stage. Entry is no longer determined by prior qualifications, nor by the ability to complete in a pre-determined time and place a course whose level and mode of study have been set by others. Ability to benefit implies potentially universal access, a 'college education for all' (British Petroleum 1989).

Targets

An elastic definition of higher education means that targets for access will also be elastic. This is unsatisfactory, but no more so than the Robbins principle for access which gave a misleading precision to the idea of an applicant's being 'qualified' or not for higher education. The distribution of the potential for higher education is arguably more continuous than dichotomous.

How, then, do we specify access targets? One view might be that this is not the time to ask the question; that the important thing is that everyone at the moment agrees that access must increase, but each for different reasons; and that it is the very vagueness of targets that has preserved this unlikely consensus. Alternatively, one criterion for setting access targets is the needs of the labour market. But here the arguments have not changed since the FHE1 report. The recent six-department review stressed again the uncertainties of forecasting labour-market demands, and no one was disturbed by the conclusion that, for the foreseeable future, 'there was a reasonably close match between overall demand and supply' (Interdepartmental Review 1990, p. 55). Another view is that, with the advent of a market in students, we would be wrong to look for a single principle, whether to reaffirm Robbins or to replace it. It is true that there must be some principle to guide public interventions in the market in respect of funding, regulation of standards, and manpower requirements. But it is not clear that higher education institutions must limit themselves to the targets implied: witness the expansion of public-sector higher education in the first half of the 1980s (Wagner 1989).

This is to think about access in terms of volume or increased access. In terms of equity, or wider access, the arguments are different and have received less attention. It seems probable that a larger and more differentiated higher education system will also be more stratified in terms both of esteem and of clientele. As we move towards the universal access implied by the idea of ability to benefit from higher education, inequalities of access will become less important, but inequalities of participation and outcome more so. Where they conflict, however, it must surely be right to give the principle of increased access priority over that of wider access. In an unexpanded system of higher education, the equalization of the social composition of the student body would do nothing for most people. It is much better to expand the chances of access for under-represented groups, even if between-group relativities are left untouched. This does not, however, mean that inequities are unimportant. Social inequities are offensive in themselves; they are inefficient and waste talent; and they usually mean that the disadvantaged are subsidizing the advantaged. For all these reasons, it remains important to establish targets for wider access. But they must be expressed in terms of outflows from groups, not simply in terms of inflows to institutions. And, as the idea of higher education itself becomes elastic, so the idea of 'access' must be extended from its present focus on initial entry to comprehend some notion of sustained and successful participation.

Traditional and non-traditional provision

One effect of an improving API is that we sharpen inequality between the young, who have had generous access to expanding provision, and the old who have not. By expanding non-traditional routes, however, we may increase and widen access for older students (among others), but only or mainly in the less esteemed areas of an increasingly differentiated tertiary system. This is one reason why it is important to integrate traditional and non-traditional forms of provision. Another reason, as Tight (1989) has argued, is that the young may well benefit from the extension to them of types of provision initially developed in relation to the not-so-young. Despite the evidence of a rising QLI and API, there is a clear need for substantial improvements throughout the UK in the pre-tertiary system of schools and colleges. Increasingly in higher education too, the modes of entry, participation and exit appropriate to older people may also be better suited to the young, perhaps especially when a market system both obliges and enables more young people to work their way through college.

FHE1 recognized the need to reform provision for sixteen- to eighteen-year-olds but concentrated on tertiary reform. The case for pre-tertiary reform, however, has since been repeatedly made, most recently in reports on behalf of British Petroleum (Smithers and Robinson 1989), the Royal Society of Arts (Ball 1990) and the Institute for Public Policy Research (IPPR) (Finegold *et al*. 1990). All advocate replacing the A level with a system that increases pupil and student choice, that rewards success, that provides attainable short-term goals which can accumulate in a variety of ways, and that reduces or dissolves the academic/vocational distinction. With the partial exception of this last consideration, all are features that are emphasized more in the traditional Scottish system. One explanation of Scotland's higher participation rates is that the Scottish system offers more types of certification, more finely adjusted to attainment after one post-compulsory year as well as after two years. Scottish provision for sixteen-to eighteen-year olds already incorporates in some degree practices move often found in provision for adults: modularization, progression and criterion referencing. Moreover, by providing the opportunity for terminal certification after a one-year post-compulsory year as well as after two years, the Scottish system recognizes what is perhaps the cardinal principle of adult provision, namely the separation of age from stage or level (McPherson *et al*. 1990; Raffe 1991).

At the time of writing, the survival of this principle has been thrown into question by the government's appointment of a committee charged with a review of post-compulsory school provision in Scotland. One proposal currently under consideration by the committee is the removal of the opportunity to take the Higher after only one post-compulsory year. But, in the evidence submitted to the committee, there are also indications of a widespread Scottish consensus that would retain existing features of Scottish provision and develop them into a fully integrated system for sixteen- to eighteen-year olds similar to that suggested in the recent IPPR report. Meanwhile, in the development of the Advanced Supplementary examination in England and Wales, and in the recent recommendations of the Schools Examination and Assessment Council, one can see a number of these 'Scottish' principles struggling to get out of the straight-jacket of the GCE A level structure (SEAC 1990).

Conclusion

By and large, the access lobby in the 1980s ignored the problems of the pre-tertiary system and advocated non-traditional solutions aimed at non-traditional students. But the need now is to engage the creative vitality of this movement across traditional provision as well. Traditional routes to higher education are neither so entrenched nor so unproductive that they can be disregarded. Their buoyancy in the 1980s weakened the development of non-traditional access, and it is only a matter of years now until the demographic upturn of the mid 1990s threatens it further. If the advance of the access movement is to be sustained, it must base itself, not at the margins of the traditional system, but at the centre where, by international standards of access and participation, it is needed no less.

4

Access and Institutional Change

Elizabeth Reid

Introduction

When the first programme of Leverhulme seminars was held a decade ago, the argument for increased access to higher education had not yet been won and the means of achieving it were still uncertain. The access seminar concentrated on making the case for a substantial increase in the participation rate on the grounds of national economic need and social justice (Fulton 1981b).

It also proposed that, in view of the forecast decline in the eighteen-year-old age group, initiatives should be taken to increase the participation in higher education of those from non-traditional backgrounds. In addition, the seminar recognized that, as well as winning the policy debate at government and institutional level, real change in institutional practice would be necessary, particularly in relation to admissions criteria, course organization and credit transfer.

The discussion on access did not systematically distinguish between increased access in the sense of making more higher education available to greater numbers of students, and wider access in the sense of the creation of a less homogeneous student population drawn from all social groups. In part, this was due to the experience of the 1970s during which the participation rate remained static and it appeared that increasing or even simply maintaining numbers in higher education inevitably entailed proposals for the recruitment of mature and non-standard entry students from a variety of socio-economic backgrounds. It was also asserted that the pool of school leavers with two A level passes was limited, although this was certainly not a judgement about ability levels in the population as a whole, but rather a view about the likely achievements of the secondary education system.

It is now better understood that there is a difference between increased access and wider access and that increased access will not of itself achieve wider access without the policies and the will to do so. However, increased access is a precondition of wider access. In Sir Christopher Ball's words, 'without the former it will be impossible to achieve the latter, because access by competition to a scarce good always favours the privileged'. (Ball 1990, p. 35)

The 1980s

In the first half of the 1980s the government argued that overall higher education provision should be rationalized and concentrated as the numbers of eighteen-year-olds declined, and it expressed concern that numbers of mature and non-standard entry students should be limited lest quality be diluted. The Green Paper *The Development of Higher Education into the 1990s* (DES 1985) published in May 1985 incorporated these views and the later publication in November 1986, *Projections of Demand for the Higher Education in Great Britain 1986–2000* (DES 1986) provided two projections of future student numbers. The government favoured Projection P, the lower of the two, which envisaged that the proportion of qualified eighteen-year-olds entering higher education would remain constant, as would entry rates for mature students. The alternative, higher projection, Projection Q, envisaged that the proportions would increase. Projection P was substantially challenged on grounds subsequently accepted by the government and the publication in 1987 of the White Paper *Higher Education: Meeting the Challenge* (DES 1987) marked a decisive change in government policies for higher education and set out a commitment to plan for an increase in participation rates and for wider access to higher education by more mature entrants and those without traditional A level qualifications. The government announced that it would plan on the basis of Projection Q on the expectation that its policies for schools and further education colleges would achieve a higher proportion of young people qualified for higher education. Thus the government endorsed routes other than A level for higher education entry, notably vocational qualifications such as BTEC, as well as access courses, as recognized routes into higher education. In accepting Projection Q the government had regard to evidence that young people whose parents were graduates were more likely to apply for and obtain places in higher education, as well as evidence of employers' requirements for highly qualified manpower.

The White Paper recognized that the consequence of this was that entry criteria and procedures would have to be changed and teaching methods and course design altered in order to provide new opportunities. The White Paper also acknowledged that there was no evidence that standards are impaired by the admission of students through access routes and that courses would benefit from the admission of access students. Credit transfer schemes and the assessment and accreditation of prior leaving were encouraged as a means of extending opportunities. The White Paper recorded the extent to which unit costs were estimated to have fallen in the 1980s (by 5 per cent in the universities and 15 per cent in the polytechnics and colleges) but went on to make clear that increased access would require further efficiency gains.

Following the passage of the Education Reform Act in 1988, separate funding councils were established for the universities and the polytechnics and colleges sector to allocate funds to institutions and to provide advice to the Secretary of State.

The Polytechnics and Colleges Funding Council sector

For the public sector, the Polytechnics and Colleges Funding Council (PCFC) has responded to the Secretary of State's guidance, issued just prior to the Council's incorporation in the autumn of 1988.

> Polytechnics and colleges have a proud record of opening pathways to higher education for those who would not otherwise have received it. In future, all higher education institutions will need to attract and recruit more students with a wider range of academic and practical experience than before, and to build on their recent success in increasing parti- cipation by women and to draw in more people from the ethnic minor- ities. Many of these will be mature students and some will not have the traditional qualifications for entry (Baker 1988).

PCFC's *Guide to the Aims and Objectives of the Council*, published in 1990, following consultation with the sector, stated that the Council would promote in the years up to 1993, *inter alia*, the objective of 'increased participation by students of all types and especially by members of groups which are under- represented in higher education' (PCFC 1990a).

The Council has been significantly successful in persuading the sector, through its funding methodology and with the aid of the government's fees policy, to increase access to higher education provided by the sector. Thus in 1989/90 student numbers increased in the polytechnics by 9 per cent and by a further 8.3 per cent in 1990/91. In November 1990, the Council, in pursuit of its overall aim to widen access, asked institutions in the sector to provide details of their plans to widen participation by women, ethnic minorities, disabled students and students from a broad range of social backgrounds, and to indicate how the implementation and progress of their plans would be monitored.

It has already been noted that simply increasing the numbers participating in higher education will not of itself widen access. Conventional demand is buoyant, at least for the time being, and factors such as the successful introduction of GCSE and the role of further education appear to be contri- buting to this previously unanticipated phenomenon. Furthermore, in the public sector unit costs continue to be reduced, and substantially increased higher education provision no longer seems unaffordable as assumptions about its financing and cost are debated and changed.

The prospects for wider access

However, notwithstanding the policy objectives of the government and PCFC, will wider access become a reality, if it no longer appears necessary to balance a decline in conventional demand from those groups already strongly represented in higher education?

At institutional level, lecturing and support staff, often as small groups of committed individuals, have undertaken a wide range of access initiatives and what is often referred to as the 'access community' or 'access movement' has become an established feature of public sector higher education. During the past decade the number of access courses has increased substantially and consortia of institutions have been established with the purpose of facilitating wider access. In 1989, following an invitation from the Secretary of State, CNAA and CVCP jointly established an Access Course Recognition Group (ACRG). The ACRG now authorizes validating agencies (individual institutions or consortia) to approve access courses as suitable for providing a basis for admission to higher education.

However, despite the greater recognition now afforded to 'access', there is evidence that access initiatives remain outside the mainstream of institutional programmes and that there are few systematic attempts to evaluate outcomes and to develop whole institutional policies for wider access.

The proceedings volume of the Society for Research into Higher Education (SRHE) conference in 1989 held at the Polytechnic of North London (Fulton 1989) recorded the conclusion that, although it was no longer necessary to argue the case for an expanded higher education system and for wider access in principle, it was more than ever necessary for institutions to change. Higher education remained an elite system:

- the participation rate was little higher than in 1970;
- most entry criteria were still based on A levels;
- curriculum and teaching methods had scarcely changed;
- students' backgrounds and expectations had scarcely changed.

The picture is not, however, uniform and by 1990 it was clear that most polytechnics and colleges had achieved some success in both increasing and widening access, albeit at the expense of a declining unit of resource, without loss of quality. The question now is how to do better.

It is the view of the PCFC that this is a matter for institutions to determine, in the light of their own circumstances. This is a widely held position. One Polytechnic director puts it thus:

The importance of institutional initiative is reflected in the many national reports which direct the bulk of their recommendations to institutions and institutional leaders. The importance of the institutional dimension can be seen by the very different behaviour of neighbouring institutions in the same urban environment and working within the same national context of policy. That policy may make it easier or harder for institutions to do what they want, but what institutions want to do is still of paramount importance. (Wagner 1989, p. 160)

Institutional change

The published papers of the Polytechnic of North London (PNL) conference include a contribution by Professor Chris Duke entitled 'Creating the Accessible Institution'. That paper provides a list of items, which taken together as 'a bundle of activities and policy initiatives' could create a more accessible institution. (Duke 1989, p. 168)

This brief paper takes up the concept of the accessible institution and considers what steps might be taken by institutional managers to make that a widespread reality. It is written from the perspective of a manager in a PCFC institution and outlines a practical and sequential approach to widening access at institutional level.

1 *A strategy for communication*

The evidence suggests that most British higher education institutions are conservative and that their staff are resistant to change (this is not necessarily a criticism, nor is it unique to higher education). In the PCFC sector there is now a particular opportunity to achieve institutional change which can be and is being seized. Managers at all levels have to ensure that lecturing and support staff understand and act upon the national and sectoral policy and resource environments. Thus energy is being devoted in institutions to ensuring that all staff are aware of the absolute necessity of achieving target student recruitment numbers, and where practical exceeding them, if the institution's income and credibility is to be secured. Growth has become a central institutional aim and the financial incentives for growth are beginning to be understood at all levels. Equal energy needs to be expended to ensure that the government's and PCFC's intention that recruitment patterns will be changed is also understood. Different attitudes towards the apparent constraints of physical capacity will increasingly be required and a more flexible approach to student attendance patterns will need to be encouraged.

At the time of writing, it appears likely that the decline in the eighteen-year-old age group in the early 1990s will be offset by a continuing rise in the participation rate. Thus, one of the most potentially powerful incentives to achieve wider access – the need to 'replace' traditional students with mature and non-standard entry students – may not materialize. However, intervention by the PCFC to promote wider access, particularly if later backed up by resource allocation procedures, could also be significant. The message at institutional level needs to be that accessibility must become a key institutional aim, that access initiatives are not 'fringe' or 'special' activities but part of the mainstream programme, not simply as an abstract and expensive good, but as a matter of institutional security and perhaps survival (in the event that the participation rate amongst eighteen-year olds falters or even declines for reasons not yet foreseen). In this way wider access becomes the policy of enlightened self-interest. It is a positive response to national and sectoral policy imperatives and a hedge against future change in patterns of student take-up. The message of demographic trends and of national and sectoral policies must be communicated vigorously. This message is an important agent of change. Clear communication will allow a wide variety of staff engaged in activities relevant to the concept of the accessible institution to understand the links and relationships between these activities. It will stimulate integration and place an appropriate public value on what may currently be discrete and isolated activities and initiatives.

This will be particularly important in those institutions previously maintained or assisted by LEAs with well developed equal opportunity policies, where there may be a need to counter a perception that wider access policies are no longer so important or relevant to the institution's mission and its funding prospects. It needs to be clearly understood in those cases that LEA policy requirements have been replaced by those of PCFC and central government. The task of communication will be correspondingly harder in those institutions which had no such LEA policy to respond to.

At every level, in its planning and objective setting processes, the institution will need clearly to convey to all its staff that wider access is as important as increased access. The title of the RSA report *More Means Different* becomes an apt slogan – the intention is not simply to recruit *more* students but *different* students. This is not an easy matter when there is a widespread view that funding for higher education is inadequate and, in the PCFC sector, that economy and efficiency have been pushed to the limit.

Funding incentives are important, but to quote the RSA report again, 'there are other keys to change, notably the creation of plans, the assertion of will, adjustment of attitudes and confrontation of inert tradition'. (Ball 1990, p. 31).

2 *The access audit*

All institutions are currently engaged in access related activities, although they may not be linked together or organized within a coherent strategy.

In 1988, HMI found that polytechnics and colleges rarely had written policies on access and that initiatives to widen access, 'tend to be *ad hoc*, disparate and uncoordinated and are often inadequately underpinned by wider institutional policy'. (DES 1989b, p. 2).

Examples of access related activities include the following:

- strong local links, particularly with neighbouring LEAs and employers;
- access links with FE colleges and adult education providers;

- membership of an open college or access consortium;
- provision of education advice and counselling in the community;
- a coherent, open and well publicized institutional admissions policy;
- recruitment objectives for under-represented groups;
- equal opportunities policies in education and employment;
- special needs provision for physically and sensorily disabled students;
- child care facilities;
- student support, e.g. counselling, study skills provision, ESL and numeracy provision;
- flexible course structures, e.g. a range of modes of attendance, different exit levels and deferred choice.

The next step, therefore, is for institutional managers to identify and map all the activities and initiatives that in any way are relevant to the goal of wider access. The examples given above are purely illustrative and there are many other possibilities. Much good staff development, for instance, will seek to improve teaching skills and that is evidently supportive of wider access. It is only by this process of identifying and describing current activity that managers can develop policy, ensure co-ordination and plan for the future.

The institutional audit will also carry the key message that all activities tending to support and secure wider access are valued and important; it will in part be a vehicle for vital communication.

3 *The whole institution policy*

Following such an audit, institutions would be better placed to develop policies for widening access. A policy for wider access would draw on the results of the audit and articulate the relationship between the different strands of activity at the different levels and within the different parts of the institution. There would be clear arrangements for promulgating the policy, both internally and externally and its 'ownership' by all groups within the institution could be secured through wide-ranging discussion during its committees and the board of governors. It might also be the subject of external consultation with a variety of interest groups. It would be formally adopted by the board of governors and set within the institution's mission and its implementation would be monitored by means of an annual statistical and evaluative report.

The policy-making process would have the important effect of bringing together, perhaps in new relationships, staff already committed in their day-to-day work to the principles of the accessible institution. It should mark the beginning of a changed culture by creating and empowering a new grouping of staff, oriented to wider access, that crosses established departmental and administrative boundaries.

4 *An action plan for wider access*

A policy has to be translated into action, however. Objectives must be set, resources allocated and timescales determined. A valuable source of ideas and recommendations is the report of the NAB Equal Opportunities Group which was set up to identify barriers to access to public sector higher education in England (NAB 1988). There is no need for institutions to labour to re-invent the wheel. What remains is for institutions to determine their own next steps, in the light of their different starting points and within their unique mission statements and polices.

The main features of the action plan, for many institutions, might incorporate the following:

a) *An improved student data-base* to cover applications, enrolments and outcomes, and provision for the analysis of this data on an annual basis so
   that trends over time can be monitored and recruitment objectives accor-
   dingly modified. Such a data-base would provide analyses by course and
   other categories relating to individual institutional organization. It would
   reveal areas of weakness and could be used to identify action points.
   PCFC sector institutions are in future to be required to produce performance indicators which measure progress towards institutional and sectoral
   aims and objectives. This is another case in which external requirements
   can be harnessed in pursuit of institutional change. It will be essential
   that institutions develop their own performance indicators in this, as in
   other areas.
b) *A coherently managed and organized student support service*, effectively publicized.
   Possible elements include:
   • induction programme;
   • study skills programme;
   • special needs support;
   • childcare;
   • education counselling during the course;
   • personal counselling and advice on finance, welfare and accommoda-
     tion;
   • careers advice.
c) *An open admissions policy* to include:
   • targeting of under-represented groups at institutional, faculty and
     course level;
   • assessment and accreditation of prior learning.
   This must be underpinned by an effective recruitment strategy, centrally directed. It will require regular staff development on policy and
   practice for senior and middle managers and admissions tutors. Current available evidence suggests that this is essential if informal departmental objectives are not to override formal institutional policy.
   (Fulton and Ellwood, 1989).

d) *Flexible course programmes* to provide for:
  - credit accumulation and transfer;
  - different modes of attendance and switches from one to another;
  - advanced standing entry;
  - different exit points appropriately certificated.
e) *A relevant staff development policy* to include:
  - enhancement of pedagogical skills;
  - development of new learning strategies;
  - appropriate course design and organization;
  - dissemination of good practice within the institution.
f) *Appropriate recruitment, selection and promotion policies*:
  - recruitment of female, black and other ethnic minority staff;
  - recruitment of staff with relevant experience outside higher education;
  - career structure to provide incentives to widening access, with promoted posts to be available not just for administration or research excellence, but also for excellence in teaching and activities which facilitate wider access.

These lists are not exclusive, nor, in most cases, could these desirable ends be achieved quickly or without controversy and expenditure. However, the essence of the action plan approach is that it prioritizes, on a year-by-year basis, those activities necessary to create an accessible institution. It provides for an annual programme of objectives within a larger framework of aims to be achieved over a period of years.

5 *Resourcing the change*

It is often said that resource constraints inhibit wider access. Access is seen as an expensive activity to support and there is frequent recourse to the argument that if the government and PCFC will the end, then they must will the means. This argument cannot entirely be sustained if an incremental programme of change is adopted. Resources can be moved at the margins each year towards modest, small-scale objectives. This requires a continuing and unrelenting scrutiny of expenditure patterns, so that activities that are no longer necessary or of sufficient propriety are stopped. Other priority activities may be resourced differently, also releasing funds for wider access objectives. Relatively small sums of money can be spent to considerable advantage in setting up activities, which once begun, will find it easier to attract resources in the following financial year. A start might be made by costing all the activities identified in the institutional audit and identifying a real-terms percentage increase in expenditure which might become a target for the following year. This could be achieved in varying proportions by a redeployment of existing resources and external income generation to replace funds diverted to access objectives.

6 *Managing the change*

The sequence of steps described cannot be achieved without direction and purposeful management. Unless the most senior managers in the institution assume responsibility for the direction and co-ordination of what might be described as 'the accessible institution programme', then access, in some institutions at least, will remain outside the mainstream. This may require some review of existing management structures and will certainly require good teamwork in the directorate to achieve consistency across the range of institutional programmes. Existing and new activities have to be measured by the simple test of whether it makes the institution more or less accessible. The complexity of the task of co-ordination requires an overview and institutions should consider identifying a senior manager (within the top three or four) to take responsibility for 'the accessible institution programme'.

Conclusion and summary

This paper recommends a six part strategy for institutions to follow:

1. A communications strategy to ensure that wider access is understood as a key institutional aim.
2. A systematic audit of access-related activities.
3. A whole-institution policy for widening access.
4. An annual action plan of achievable objectives to increase access.
5. An annual financial target for access-related expenditure.
6. Identification of a senior manager with responsibility for the 'accessible institution programme'.

Taken together, these six propositions should provide a straightforward and practical approach to widening access at institutional level. They build on present and foreseeable national and sectoral requirements and incorporate elements of good management practice that are increasingly being adopted within institutions.

5

Access: An Overview

Peter Scott

Ten years ago in FHE1 the first topic to be discussed was the labour market. A decade later access has pride of place. That priority is deserved. Access is the fundamental issue in the shaping of future higher education policy. The degree of access determines the overall size and shape of the system; it delineates questions of academic quality and institutional governance (clearly these questions are much more pressing and also more complicated in a wide-open than in a closed system); and it is at the heart of the debate about how higher education should be funded. Everything flows back to access.

Not only has the focus of higher education policy shifted during the 1980s from the labour market to access, from manpower planning to wider opportunities, but an equally significant shift has taken place during the same period in the way that the question of wider access is perceived. At the start of the 1980s many people believed that higher education would be hit hard by demographic decline. Successive policy papers and student number projections from the Department of Education and Science suggested that there would be a serious shortfall of students in the depths of the demographic trough in the early and middle 1990s. These detailed predictions seemed to confirm the general impression that after two decades of headlong growth the Robbins expansion was running out of steam.

Against this background of falling demand from school leavers and other conventional entrants for higher education places it was felt that the salvation of the system lay with 'Access' – that is, the increased recruitment of non-standard students. Two major sources were identified, older students (many of them women who might want to study part-time) and able young adults who had failed to gain the standard qualifications for entry to higher education because of a deficient or interrupted secondary education but who, nevertheless, could be brought up to standard by means of special 'Access' programmes. And there were two main motives for this growing interest in 'Access'. The first was the desire to maintain student numbers at a time when it was anticipated that demand from standard school leavers would rapidly decline, thereby ensuring the survival of courses, departments and institutions which otherwise might have to close. In plain language, self-interest. The second was the urge to reach out to help the educationally disadvantaged and the socially deprived. This crusade for equal opportunities seemed to many to be the extension of the liberal goals of the new universities and the popular ambitions of the polytechnics. In other words, altruism with just a dash of a less worthy paternalism. But, whether the motive was selfish or altruistic, it was widely assumed that wider access could only be achieved against the grain of higher education.

Today the perception is very different. Despite the decline in the number of eighteen-year-olds in the general population, demand from standard school leavers is buoyant. In successive years the number of students enrolled by polytechnics and colleges of higher education has increased by almost seven per cent and then by a further ten per cent. Growth in universities, although less rapid, has also been marked. Of course recruitment difficulties persist in less popular subjects like mechanical engineering and the shortage of good mathematics and physics teachers in schools continues to depress the demand for student places in natural sciences. But few institutions fear a serious shortfall of students during the 1990s. And at the levels of sectors and the system as a whole the pressing difficulties now seem to be those of capacity not of demand.

A number of reasons have been offered to explain this remarkable turn-around, from anticipated bust to actual boom. The first, and probably the most significant, is that the children of those who were sucked into higher education during the great expansion of the 1960s are now leaving school and seeking university or polytechnic places. The strongest indicator of the propensity to enter higher education has always been the possession of graduate parents. So the growing number of graduate parents provides a built-in accelerator of future student demand. A second reason, which has received much recent attention, is the success of the new General Certificate of Secondary Education (GCSE) in England and Wales which has encouraged many more sixteen-year-olds to stay on into school sixth forms or continue their studies at colleges, so making themselves available for higher education entry. This is a powerful factor certainly because only with the introduction of the GCSE, an examination designed for all sixteen-year-olds rather than only the academically able, has the promise of secondary education for all set out in the 1944 Education Act finally been realized.

A third reason is the success of comprehensive reorganization of secondary education which has had a similar effect. For the first time the mass of school pupils, rather than the academic select, has become, even notionally, eligible to enter higher education. This explains the strange paradox that comprehensive schools have frequently been criticized for lowering standards while in fact expanding their output of acceptable higher education candidates by almost three times over the past two decades. A fourth reason, plainly, is the changing condition of women in British society. One of the most powerful factors in the expansion of higher education during the 1970s and 1980s was increased participation by women. No doubt this reflected a far-reaching equalization of opportunities for women and men. In practical terms parents began to have the same ambitions for their daughters as for their sons, while largely female professions like teaching and nursing made increasing efforts to secure either an all-graduate status or, at the very least, a much heavier graduate mix. Clearly as female participation approaches parity with male there will be less scope for securing extra growth by these means. A final, more speculative, reason is that the 1980s have been (or have appeared to be) a prosperous decade. Real living standards have risen and with them expectations not only of material goods but also of 'cultural' goods, like higher education. Although deplored by many people in the system attached to older idealistic notions, higher education has taken on many of the attributes of a desirable commodity. This changed perception of its social worth has also increased student demand.

Widening access to higher education is no longer conceived at the start of the 1990s as a crusade to help the educationally and socially deprived, to reach out into the depths of Britain's democracy (and, incidentally, to save departments and institutions from threatened closure!). Instead it is seen in much less heroic terms, as the careful management of burgeoning demand mainly, but not exclusively, from standard school leavers and other conventional sources. 'Access' in its early 1980s sense seems to have been superseded by 'demand'. Of course it is a mistake to imagine too sharp a dichotomy. The fact that middle-class girls now have access to higher education on terms that approach those for middle-class boys is a considerable social advance.

However, the most important question that must be asked about this shifting view of access is whether today's perception of the issue is an accurate one. After all, the strong sense of demographic doom that pervaded the policy discussions of the early 1980s has turned out to be misplaced; it is at least possible that the present sense of buoyant demand may prove to be equally misplaced. Although recent increases in enrolments have been impressive, they are only a small beginning in the larger context of moving the Age Participation Index from below a fifth to above a quarter. And sensations of social and economic well-being can quickly dissolve when faced with the urgent and ugly fact of recession. A second cautionary note has already been mentioned. The near-equalization of male and female participation means that there is limited scope to further increase student numbers by raising female enrolment. A third qualification is also necessary. As was noted earlier, demand is not equally strong across all disciplines, institutions and sectors. Serious shortfalls may still occur, although many institutions have developed sophisticated strategies for equalizing student demand. A good example is engineering courses that have been nudged in their subject matter closer to computing and business studies, both areas of buoyant demand. So, although the present perception that student demand is likely to stay buoyant through the 1990s is probably substantially correct, there remain detailed problems to do with the distribution of demand.

Nor can demand be considered in isolation from supply. During the 1980s unit costs have been reduced, sharply so in the case of the polytechnics and colleges and significantly so in that of the universities. Many people in higher education regret this squeeze on unit costs and remain concerned about its longer-range effect on academic quality, particularly if it continues unabated in the 1990s. Adjusting to lower levels of resourcing has often been a bruising experience and occasionally a traumatic one. Because of the inflexible cost structure of higher education this squeeze has brought some institutions to a point of acute financial crisis. At least twelve universities have been included on a 'worry list' drawn up by the Universities Funding Council. Although the Polytechnics and Colleges Funding Council has no equivalent list, it is no secret that there are institutions at risk in the non-university sector too. But, despite all this, it has to be accepted that by driving down unit costs in the 1980s the government has made it easier to contemplate rapid expansion in the 1990s – if only because the inevitable objections of the Treasury have been reduced. In the short run the 1981 cuts in university budgets, remembered as a traumatic episode, were bad in terms of demand, because fewer places were available for students; but in the longer run and in supply-side terms it can be argued they had a beneficial effect, because they began the difficult process of reducing unit costs. A similar argument can be constructed in relation to two-year degrees. Whatever the academic objections to this foreshortening of degrees, their introduction would also have the effect of easing supply-side difficulties by lowering the overall cost per graduate.

Two important questions are raised by these changing perceptions of student demand. First, will the lessening concern about the ability of institutions to fill their places during the demographic trough during the early and middle 1990s discourage reform and experiment? Until a few years ago the fear was that unless higher education modified its practices to appeal to a wider student constituency courses would close, departments merge and entire institutions be threatened because they would be unable to recruit students. The urge to open up and reform the system was powerfully reinforced by self-interest. And it was by appealing to this self-interest that reformers were able to convince their more conservatively inclined colleagues about the need for change. In the new climate, that will be much more difficult because there appears to be buoyant demand from standard students. The desire seems to be for more not for different higher education. So during the 1990s one of the most powerful motives for supporting the reform of the system may become less persuasive. Second, will the now independent polytechnics and colleges of higher education be willing or able to sustain the same commitment to special access programmes in which the local education authorities which formerly maintained them had taken a particular interest? The one area in which many authorities took a positive (as opposed to negative) interest in their polytechnics and colleges was in the field of special access programmes and equal opportunities policies. Already one influential observer has detected signs of this area receiving lower priority in the mission statements of some PCFC institutions.

Such arguments, however, rest on the assumption that there is a conflict between 'Access' and access, that special programmes to widen access for non-standard students thrive when demand from standard students appears to dwindle and that when conventional demand picks up again such programmes are given much less emphasis. And this assumption depends in turn on a view of a *noblesse oblige* higher education, an essentially elitist system that nevertheless reaches out to help the outcasts of post-school education. But it may be that there is no necessary conflict between non-standard 'Access' and standard access. Perhaps it is only when middle-class participation in higher education approaches saturation level that working-class participation is like to expand on a serious scale. Certainly the experience of the United States suggests that a higher education system that enrols mass school-leaver intakes is also a system that is open to adult returners, the educationally and socially disadvantaged and other kinds of non-standard student. But there is a risk that, although in the long run these two views of access are complementary rather than competitive, those who campaign for more democratic access to British higher education in the next few years may find it more difficult to be heard in the absence of any serious fears about a famine of standard entrants.

Whatever form wider access takes it is likely to involve further education as heavily as higher education – which makes it especially ironic that the new arrangements for the government and management of the latter made under the Education Reform Act have created a sharper distinction between 'advanced' and 'non-advanced' further education. This distinction will make less and less sense as the 1990s proceed. At present higher education's interest in further education is limited, although FE colleges now produce more A level candidates than school sixth forms. Britain is still far behind the United States where the FE college equivalent, the community college, is recognized as part of the higher education system. However, far-reaching changes are already at work. Further education has already 'invaded' the final two years of secondary education through formal and informal tertiary arrangements. It is possible that during the next decade further education may 'invade' the early years of higher education. This invasion could take a variety of forms – special access programmes with dedicated entry to the neighbouring university or polytechnic; franchising deals under which the first or even second years of degree courses were undertaken in the more economical environment of further education; interwoven patterns of education and training shared between higher and further education institutions in a genuine partnership, perhaps based on pre-packaged modules that could also be used for distance learning; much closer collaboration in continuing education, particularly in the post-experience field. Many of these innovations are already being put into practice.

These closer links with further education are likely to increase the interest in two-year foundation degrees which could either be 'topped up' by two more years of academic study or perhaps one of professional training. It will be argued that such an arrangement would fit in better with the emerging pattern of post-school education. Two-year degrees would certainly help to loosen up the supply-side difficulties which continue to inhibit wider access. To the extent that the introduction of shorter first degrees drove down unit costs and increased graduate throughput it would have a similar effect to the reduction of unit costs during the 1980s. To that extent it is right to link two-year degrees with wider access. But those who support their introduction must first answer two questions. First, why replace one rigid formula, the three- or four-year honours degree, with another, the two-year foundation degree? If introduced on a significant scale the latter would inevitably replace the former as the standard currency of higher education, especially if student support (whether in the form of grants or loans) were to be confined to the first two years of higher education. Two-year degrees would be likely to be socially divisive because privileged students would no doubt continue onto the second cycle of higher education while the less privileged left after two years with their foundation degrees. And they would also offer much less room for academic manoeuvre. Already there are complaints that it is difficult to combine breadth and depth in an intensive degree pattern like the English. This task would become even more difficult if two-year foundation degrees were established as higher education's standard.

Second, would two-year degrees be able to reproduce the intellectual coherence of most honours degrees? Degree, it must be remembered, are academic as well as administrative categories. However flexible their arrangement of options or modular structure, they associate knowledge and skills in subtle and particular ways. They cannot easily be chopped into pieces and put back together in a different order. They can only be rearranged by paying the closest attention to the inner rhythms of disciplines, groups of disciplines or professional fields of study. Of course coherent two-year qualifications can be successfully designed. The Higher National Diploma is a good example, although its academic 'feel' is different from that of an honours degree. But it is not easy, as the uncertain development of the Diploma of Higher Education has demonstrated. So advocates of two-year foundation degrees must make out an intellectual as well as a socio-economic case for their usefulness. So far this has not been seriously attempted. This is a serious deficiency in the wider debate about a move towards mass access. Although it is sometimes assumed that the three- or four-year honours degree is a barrier to broader access because it appears intimidating to non-standard students, there is little evidence to support this assumption. Non-standard students seem to crave a standard higher education. This suggests that the question of wider access cannot simply be reduced to matters of costs and structures or even of degree content; it goes very much wider, powerfully reverberating the instincts and intentions of our culture in its widest sense as well as being shaped by, and shaping, the contours of post-industrial society and impulses of democratic life. In other words access cannot be understood from within the higher education world but only from the outside looking in. This is hardly surprising because, as was argued at the beginning of this short paper, access is the system's most fundamental issue and characteristic.

6

Governance and Sectoral Differentiation

William H. Stubbs

Introduction

Structure and governance were the topics for the last of the nine publications which formed FHE1. The recommendations of this part of the study were introduced succinctly in these words of Michael Shattock:

> the structure and governance of higher education are never likely to be discussed in Britain in terms of abstract principles. Historically there has always been a strong tendency to see higher education in terms of a hierarchy of institutions and to allot status to types of institutions without defining whether that status derives from academic quality, funding or social prestige. Function was always subsidiary to status. (Shattock 1983, p. 198.)

The sixteen recommendations of this part of the study are listed in Annex 1 to this chapter. Also listed are the recommendations of the Select Committee on Education, Science and the Arts which had previously considered in 1980 the organization, co-ordination and control of higher education (Annex 2). It is evident that much of FHE1 was influenced by the Select Committee's findings.

Ten years later, depending on the severity of your marking, more than half the FHE1 recommendations have been acted upon. That so many of the recommendations were directed at the problem of hierarchy evidently disappointed the chairman of the study group, Lord Crowther-Hunt. He considered the main theme to have been the future relationship between the government and the institutions – 'unless we get that relationship right the rest of the Leverhulme programme will be so much pie-in-the-sky.'

The chairman also was clear on another point:

> There is, of course, no such thing in Britain as 'natural demand' for places in higher education when the government determines the level of student grants and whether or not they should be replaced by, or

supplemented by, loans. Government decisions in this area determine, or have a major influence on, student demand.... So let's forget about concepts of natural demand. (Shattock 1983, p. 4)

These comments, which seemed eminently rational at the time, were made at the beginning of a decade which was to see a decline in real terms in the public resources for higher education and the value of the mandatory student award. During this same period the numbers of higher education students increased by over a quarter.

Changes since 1980

The major changes in governance over the last decade which derive from the 1988 Education Reform Act and the preceding White Paper *Meeting the Challenge*, are:

- the gain by the polytechnics and colleges of independent status;
- a major reduction of direct involvement by local education authorities in higher education;
- the ending of the special – or anomalous – constitutional arrangement of the UGC and the establishment of two new national funding councils.

These changes took place during a period when higher education moved further and irreversibly towards the higher participation models of the United States and Europe. Consequently, as the cost of higher education to the state increased to almost one per cent of the GDP, its contributions to society, or perhaps more accurately to the national economy, attracted more attention from political parties, government, industry and the press.

In comparison with 1980, the most significant consequences for the organization and funding of higher education have been:

- an increase in the accountability by institutions for public funds. An unspecified or unhypothecated block grant has faded as a basis of resource allocation. The provision of funds is more directly related to the numbers of students and the subjects which they are studying;
- greater freedom for institutions with respect to the numbers of students they admit. The substantial increases in tuition fees and, for colleges and polytechnics, the abolition of the course approval system, have effectively ended for most courses the concept of central control of admissions to any individual institution. Entry to medical, dentistry and, in some respects, initial teacher training remain as exceptions to the general position;
- a greater differentiation between the funds allocated for teaching and those for research. This applies more significantly to universities given the continuation of the dual funding policy for research;
- an emerging new hierarchy for universities, *de facto* if not *de jure*, along the lines of the recommendations of the Advisory Board for the Research

Councils (ABRC) regarding differentiation between three types of institutions:

Type R: Institutions offering both undergraduate and postgraduate teaching and substantial research activity across the range of fields.

Type T: Institutions highly competent in undergraduate and MSc teaching with staff engaged in the scholarship and research necessary to support and develop that teaching, but without provision of advanced research facilities.

Type X: Institutions providing teaching across a broad range of fields and engaged in substantial world class research in particular fields where they are already pre-eminent or could achieve eminence in collaboration with other institutions;

• a reduced role for university senates and college academic boards as a result of the recommendations of the Jarratt Report (CVCP 1985) and the changes introduced in the Articles of Governance of the new Higher Education Corporations and the greater prominence given to the role of the chief executive of an institution;

• greater emphasis on management skills in the running of institutions. The slow but inevitable progress in constructing meaningful performance indicators, the extension to all institutions of the requirement to prepare strategic plans, the continuing after-shocks of the consequences of the financial crisis experienced by University College (Cardiff), and the increasing competition between institutions for students and funds all combine to give increased prominence to management and leadership issues.

Issues for the 1990s

The background

The commitment to a substantial expansion of student numbers commands wide political and educational support and seems set to continue into the nineties. The expansion in numbers during the 1980s was accompanied by concerns about the provision of adequate recurrent funds to maintain an acceptable – if increasingly illusory – standard unit of funding. These concerns, which were held to more uniformly in the university sector, will no doubt continue to be heard. However, the substantial increases in the level of tuition fees are likely to prove sufficiently attractive to many institutions to result in efforts being made to enrol significant additional numbers of students without any additional central grant. At the start of this decade some 10 per cent of undergraduates at universities are admitted solely on the basis of income from tuition fees. In the PCFC sector the equivalent figure for all full-time and sandwich students is just under 14 per cent. Against this background and the changes to the management and organization which have already come about, the following issues seem likely to be prominent.

The location of expansion

The basis for the future is a national commitment and determination to achieve an expansion in the numbers of students which would double the existing numbers by early in the next century. What is less clear is where this increase will take place. In other words, will each institution of higher education see itself as expanding at a similar rate to its neighbours, thereby aiming to achieve its share of a common goal irrespective of its size, location and the demand by students? Possibly, but unlikely. Differences in ethos, popularity and reputation can be expected to have their influence. In macro terms, so to speak, it is at present an open question as to whether or not universities will generally commit themselves to expansion on the scale now envisaged without commensurate increases in funds. If the experience of the decade just ended were to be repeated through to the turn of the century, and if the polytechnics and colleges continue to attract and provide for disproportionately more students than their existing share might be considered to merit, then the higher education landscape in England and Wales will be changed significantly, and probably irreversibly, in a remarkably short period of time. The university share of the nation's undergraduate population will have become a distinctly minority one. Whether or not this change will come to pass will rest substantially on the overall level of resources made available for higher education and how they are distributed within the two sectors of higher education.

The pattern for the future will also be determined by the stance which each institution takes towards the nature of growth in student numbers. The student population of the future will not be uniform in nature. The traditional entry cohort comprises students between the age of eighteen and twenty-one who enter higher education direct from or soon after leaving secondary school or sixth form college. The diminishing size of this cohort will mitigate the effect of any increase in the proportion of these students entering higher education. In contrast, substantial real increases seem more likely in the numbers of older students who decide to enter higher education, either for the first time or to improve their existing qualifications.

And many of these students will prefer to study part-time. It is students such as these who now make up the majority of the population of polytechnics and colleges. In terms of part-time students, the difference between the two sectors is most marked. Whereas less than 3 per cent of English university undergraduate students (excluding the Open University) study part-time, 35 per cent of polytechnic and college students choose this way to obtain a qualification. For an institution to provide in any substantial and successful way for their client group, it has to be committed to organizing its courses in a manner which provides incentives and adequate flexibility to meet student choice. Progress by any institution on the motorway of expansion will, as a consequence, only be made after considering how to respond to signs on the entry roads marked 'non-standard qualifications' and 'non-traditional background'. It will also depend on the ability of those who govern institutions to respond in suitable time to the changing circumstances of student demand. Polytechnics and colleges have shown they are capable of adapting to 'environmental changes'. A question for universities will be whether their rate of evolution post-Jarratt is adequate.

Setting the scene for these changes will ultimately be a matter for the councils of universities and the governing bodies of PCFC institutions. It is for them to decide on the nature of the institutions for which they are responsible. Mission statements may have previously been seen by some as bland descriptions about the future which could be used to justify a variety of changes – or lack of change. In future, however, declarations about missions are likely to become indicators, no doubt clearer in some instances than in others, of where an institution wishes to place itself in the expanding world of higher education. The declared aims of institutions and how they set about achieving them may come to have more significance than any remaining differences in their titles.

The place of research

Decisions concerning the extent which any institution commits itself to the teaching of undergraduate and other students are related to, and in a few instances greatly influenced by, the scale and the nature of its involvement with research. There are few higher education institutions which would deny having any aspirations in this regard. No matter how small they are or how specialized is the nature of their academic programme all institutions claim to have some research activity taking place within their ranks. Research is considered to be a necessary adjunct to teaching.

For many polytechnics, there is an increasing sense of frustration that universities should have access to the benefit of a dual funding arrangement for research whereby universities receive funds both for designated research directly from the various Research Councils, and additional support as part of the general funds from their Funding Council. This dual funding of research to universities has assumed greater significance because of the advantage it is considered to give universities in maintaining a 'well founded' base, not only for research purposes but in support of their teaching – an activity which is now exceeded in volumes of students by the other institutions of higher education.

Partly in recognition of this concern, the government has sought from the Universities Funding Council greater distinction between the funds provided for teaching and those for research. At the same time, by 1993/94 some £97m of funds is due to be transferred from UFC funding to the Research Councils. Research funding is therefore to become more clearly defined and more of it made available for competition by all institutions of higher education. Research activity in universities is also becoming less uniform and is increasingly being concentrated in a limited number of institutions. A similar trend is evident with UFC funding. Partly this is in response to the increasing costs of more sophisticated equipment and partly to the increasing inter-disciplinary nature of more modern research: advances in one subject are catalyzed by proximity to teams of researchers working in related subjects.

The concentration of income to universities from the different Research Councils can be ascertained by examining the cumulative funding from each Council to each university. The Medical RC funding is most concentrated, that of the Agriculture and Food RC and Natural Environment RC less so and that of the Science and Engineering RC least concentrated. Overall the first 50 per cent of each Research Council's funds is allocated to just ten institutions. The 'top ten' institutions funded by each Council are not identical but the lists are similar. There is no indication that this trend is slowing down or being reversed.

The financial base for growth

In all phases of education the two principal determinants of expansion are the numbers of teaching staff and the capacity of the teaching accommodation – much of it of a specialist nature. Additions to either of these can be costly: on the one hand there is the pay of highly qualified and suitably experienced personnel and on the other the capital costs of building new accommodation or remodelling that which is no longer adequate for up-to-date teaching methods and changed curriculum requirements.

As there seems little prospect of resources for higher education being increased in direct proportion to the proposed increase in student numbers, the expectation will be that institutions find ways of increasing the effective deployment of their existing resources. Some of this could be achieved by using existing physical resources on an extended daily timetable over more months in the year. There also seems further scope for increasing, in some areas, the staff–student ratios – although considerable improvements have been achieved in recent years.

However, what remain to be attempted on any significant scale in most institutions are more radical changes to the organization of education, for example by reducing the time required to obtain a degree qualification, greater use of distance learning methods in conjunction with more traditional teaching methods, and more use of teaching materials produced in common with other institutions.

If changes in these methods could be introduced without seriously weakening the relationship between teacher and learner, more students than would otherwise be the case, could have access to the benefits of higher education.

Developments of both kinds – greater efficiency and increased effectiveness – will best be undertaken by institutions on their own terms. However, change will need to be accommodated in the new environment whereby it is for the governing bodies and councils to ensure that institutions do not unreasonably overextend themselves financially. Governors are now responsible in law for the solvency of their institution – and may not delegate this responsibility to others.

This increased responsibility within institutions of higher education for public funds and the accountability that accompanies it is a new feature of the governance of higher education.

In 1985 the Department of Education and Science took the exceptional step of formally intervening in the affairs of University College, Cardiff when the UGC informed the Department that the College was in financial difficulties with a substantial accumulated deficit. The shock waves from this intervention have continued to reverberate through the higher education sector.

Subsequent recommendations from the Public Accounts Committee (PAC) left little doubt of what was expected from the new Funding Councils and the institutions they fund:

> We welcome the establishment of the new Universities Funding Council, with an expanded role, a more positive remit and greater powers and responsibilities. We expect the Council to pursue vigorously its responsibilities for economy, efficiency and effectiveness in university funding, and to provide the high level of accountability to Parliament required by the very large sums of public funds for which it is now directly responsible.
>
> ... We expect the Council quickly to build up the planning arrangements, financial management and information systems, and the capacity for monitoring and analysis which are essential for the effective allocation and oversight of the grants to universities. We look to the Council to secure prompt and determined action where required by the public interest, whilst recognizing also the responsibility and autonomy of the universities themselves in such matters. The successful combination of operational autonomy with central oversight of financial performance has to be secured in many private and public sector activities; it is no less necessary in the university sector. (House of Commons 1990a, paras 24, 25)

A later Treasury minute responding to the recommendations in the PAC reports put these in the context of the responsibilities of institutions: 'neither DES nor the Universities Funding Council can underwrite the financial situation at each university' (House of Commons 1990b).

Summary

Many of the proposals for changes in the governance of higher education made in the early 1980s by FHE1 have been implemented by the end of the decade. The increased and continuing demand for higher education, and the widespread support for this across the political spectrum, will test the effectiveness of the revised arrangements. In particular, the financial implications of the extent of expansion at individual institutions and the developing character of the institution, including the provisions given to research, will be matters that seem likely to assume greater significance for those with responsibilities for the governance of colleges, polytechnics and universities.

Annex 1

The Structure and Governance of HE (FHE1)

Proposals:

1. The DES, the UGC and the NAB should recognize that the protection and encouragement of institutional self-governance and initiative through the operation of multiple sources of funding, responsiveness to external societal demands and strong local/community involvement offer the best prospect for maintaining academic innovation and creativity.
2. Greater emphasis should be given to institutional autonomy. Autonomy, however, should be regulated by agreed institutional 'mission statements' and considerations of national need and the patterns of demand. Funding should be in accordance with institutions' missions statements, which should be the subject of periodic review.
3. Representative local committees should be set up to co-ordinate and stimulate the provision of adult, continuing and post-experience education, combining the interests of institutions, LEAs and other local providers.
4. Machinery for co-operation at regional level amongst institutions of higher education should be set up by the institutions themselves to complement the closer working relationships between the UGC and the NAB recommended below (Proposal 11).
5. Priority should be given to adopting systems of course control which encourage academic initiative and speedy responses to changing student interests.
6. The UGC and the NAB should place a high priority on the need for co-operation at officer, committee/board and subject committee levels.
7. UGC and NAB advice to government should be published, as should the criteria they use to make judgements between institutions.
8. The staffing of the two bodies should be adequate to their respective remits and should be appointed independently of the DES, a majority being drawn from higher education itself.
9. Ways should be found, either by the appointment of assessors on the committee/board or at the subject committee level, of relating the legitimate interests of government departments other than the DES with the work of UGC/NAB and with the institutions of higher education, in order to ensure that institutions' research and training responsibilities take proper account of national needs.

10. The Secretary of State should continue to appoint members of the UGC, but should publish the criteria governing the selection in advance and should take the necessary decision only after consultation with the various constituencies involved, including the consumers of higher education.
11. After a five-year review period, the longer-term prospect should be for an even closer working relationship between the UGC and NAB, and these two bodies and the DES should accept this as their long-term objective.
12. UGC and NAB should include within their remit the entire higher education provision including direct grant and voluntary institutions.
13. In any future arrangements there should be a recognition and reflection of a continuing place for LEAs in tertiary education provision.
14. The role of validating bodies in the future structure of higher education needs review as their role changes in respect to the increasingly autonomous institutions in the public sector.
15. An overarching advisory body should be established to offer strategic advice to the Secretary of State on matters relating to higher education, including the division of funding. The new body should not interfere with the established powers and functions of the UGC and NAB.
16. Priority should be given to the establishment of a higher education policy studies centre to serve as an independent source of advice for the DES and other government departments as well as the UGC, NAB and the institutions of higher education themselves.

Annex 2

Report by the House of Commons Select Committee on Education, Science and Arts in 1980

This report recommended *inter alia:*

1. A Committee for Colleges and Polytechnics (CCP) should be set up by the Secretary of State to give advice and make recommendations about the finance, administration and planning of institutions in the maintained sector engaged in advance of further education.
2. The CCP, together with the UGC, should set up a joint secretariat with DES observers, to co-ordinate planning in higher education.
3. When the CCP is set up the government should bring forward proposals under which it is the duty of the UGC and the CCP to make public more information about their activities and methods of administration, and about the formal advice they submit to government.
4. The lay membership of the UGC should be increased to include further representatives of local education authorities (LEAs) and both sides of industry.

5. The government should, after a period of not less than five years and not more than ten years from the setting up of the CCP, review both its functions and those of the UGC.

6. All colleges, polytechnics and universities should submit to the UGC or the CCP, for approval, detailed statements regarding their purposes and objectives. When approved, these statements should be published and used as a 'touchstone' against which proposals for new developments should be considered.

7. The regional advisory councils should be abolished. Some of their activities, not involving higher education, may need to be continued by a smaller organization.

8. Institutions of higher education and local education authorities should co-operate on an area or sub-regional basis in voluntary planning, particularly for continuing education, and every institution of higher education should be required to publish an annual report on the extent to which facilities are being shared, and draw particular attention to unnecessary duplication.

7

Governance: The Institutional Viewpoint

Michael Richardson

Introduction

The recommendations of FHE1 on governance fell into six broad areas:

1. Institutional autonomy
2. Validation and course controls
3. Regional and local co-ordination
4. The UGC and NAB
5. Higher education governance in the late 1980s
6. The development of policy in higher education.[1]

The purpose of this chapter is to address the institutional viewpoint on developments in these areas – recognizing that every institution exists within a context which is local, regional, national and, probably increasingly, international – and to identify some cross-cutting themes.

Institutional autonomy

What is referred to in FHE1 as 'institutional self-governance and initiative' might be protected and encouraged at least as much by a strong local community involvement as it is by multiple funding sources. Likewise how is such local institutional self-governance to be responsive to external societal demands? The issues here appear to be particularly sensitive. One interpretation of the code, for example, could equate 'multiple funding sources' with decreased central governmental funding at any price regardless of the state of any particular institution's development trajectory, the needs of a local or national community's particular skills and the acknowledged 'step function' of critical investment in new technologies and staff development. Conversely, multiple funding sources can perfectly appropriately be seen as a way of broadening the base of financial support for any higher education institution and lessening its reliance upon and level of beholdenness to any given government department. An issue here which remains live is the extent to which the concept of multiple funding actually removes from government a central obligation to secure a core of appropriate funding for the higher education system.

Another aspect of the recommendations on institutional autonomy dealt with the question of mission statements. The recommendation actually set out with the words 'that greater emphasis should be given to institutional autonomy'. It then went on to say 'autonomy, however, should be regulated by agreed institutional "mission statements" and considerations of national need and the patterns of demand.' It related the funding of institutions with such mission statements and suggested there should be a periodic review. Perhaps it is reasonable to ask how the notions in this recommendation progressively moved towards the idea of contracts and the consequent, in some cases all too slavishly followed, pathways of 'programme funding'. Both the mission statement and the concept of programme funding are in themselves potentially valuable ideas. However, they do raise quite sharply some major questions. Who, for example, is capable of credibly making a judgement on a mission statement from an established higher education institution? Is it a group from within the Committee of Vice-Chancellors and Principals (CVCP) or another university? Is it a transient group of junior ministers and civil servants within a particular government department? In the absence of the kind of independent body proposed in recommendation 16 of the FHE1 volume (see p. 69), it seems all too likely that pragmatism and practice would place such judgements in the hands of those who would, through no fault of their own, have neither the background knowledge nor the experience to deliver such judgements satisfactorily.

Validation and course controls

If we move now to the area of validation and course controls we are immediately confronted by the tension between multiplicity of 'chartered' autonomous bodies and various centralized systems of validation. This tension is not yet resolved. What, for example, is the relationship between greater local autonomy in the public sector and a national maintenance of standards? Where is located the role for a national agency like the National Council for Vocational Qualifications, the responsibility for the National Forum for Management Education and Development or the Management Charter Initiative? Somewhere near the heart of this clutch of questions is the basic and uncomfortable challenge, the statement that the apparent equality between existing higher education institutions is not a reality but a myth. Has it, for example, ever been true that there is an equivalence of value of qualification from separate and separately chartered universities or that even within an apparently coherent framework called the Council for

National Academic Awards (CNAA) the value attaching to individual qualifications from disparate institutions entitled by the same names have been in
any sense equal? It is conceivable that the implementation of the higher
levels of National Vocational Qualification (NVQ) and a broadening commitment to developing the Enterprise in Higher Education initiative (EHE)
present us with mechanisms which are at least potentially both national and
in the old sense transbinary. It would be a challenge to build on these
models, but also to determine in particular how their academic credibility
would be established and safeguarded nationally.

Regional and local co-ordination

Apart from the wider political considerations of regional and local government, the issue of regional and local co-ordination of higher education is
thrown into sharp relief on a number of fronts. Two points illustrate this.
First, the dividing line between higher and further education is blurring
considerably, as at other levels in the system (for example, there are more
students following A level courses in the further education system than there
are in sixth forms). There is a significant measure of mobility within this
system. The second major factor impacting upon regional and local co-
ordination and higher education, particularly at the vocational end of the
spectrum, is the coming into being of the Training and Enterprise Councils
(TECs). Although regarded initially as yet another wheeze by a government
determined to continue to produce something new out of a hat at regular
intervals, it does appear that the TECs have taken root with the kind of
strength that their progenitors would have wished. Local enterprises in the
majority of cases have taken their creation very seriously and local educational providers on both sides of the old binary line have wished to become
involved. This at least potentially gives a sharper focus to the total local
higher education provision both in academic work and in vocational areas
than had been possible under the Regional Advisory Councils for FE,
although these councils need clearly to continue to feed into and be informed
by the work of the TECs. At the regional level the extent to which some
recent legislative changes have enhanced the competitive spirit in the balance
of territorial and recruitment interests needs to be recognized. Some aspects of
this promote a spirit of fierce and sometimes indeed divisive competition
which is both intersectoral, interinstitutional and intrasectoral, and yet some
of the same guidelines appear to advocate interinstitutional collaboration to
ensure the most cost-effective deployment of resource. The system overall, to
whomever it belongs, cannot have it both ways. Interinstitutional and intersectoral collaboration must have a pay-off for the parties to it, and a blind
and sometimes facile adherence to beliefs in market forces, coupled with a
vision that institutions provide education as a product which is in some way
similar to chocolate bars, does not further the case.

The UGC (UFC) and the NAB (PCFC)

FHE1 addressed itself to the role of the then UGC and the then NAB with regard to individual institutions. The transmogrification of the UGC and the NAB to the UFC and PCFC is now behind us. However, the issues in this group of recommendations remain pertinent, not only at a systems level. Certainly these relatively new bodies must have a central and significant role in 'advice' to government and this they do not formally have. Their formal role in advising regional components of local government on higher education issues is also important. The independence of the staffing of any regional support structure to these bodies is fundamental and needs to be visibly safeguarded. As the wider range of government departments involved centrally in issues of education and training feeds through locally, as with the funding for the Training and Enterprise Councils, mechanisms for handling locally the inter-relationship of a proliferation of government departmental interests will need to be more quickly developed.

Higher education governance

We now approach that area of FHE1 which looked forward to the late 1980s, and which prompts some hard questions. FHE1 spoke of an even closer relationship between UGC and NAB. Where do we turn for signs of this closer relationship? Is it indeed an explicit and stated commitment or objective of any government department? At a national level in what forum is the debate being conducted which continues to bring together at the appropriate level the interest of 'training' and the interests of education? Moving down again to the institutional level in what local forum is the 'continuing place of LEAs in tertiary education' being systematically examined and promoted? How can local institutions expect to benefit from any 'overarching advisory body' as suggested in recommendation 15? In one sense the relative transience of specialist junior ministers in departments of central government can be offset by a greater continuity in the governance of local institutions. None the less discontinuities of policy created centrally can impact powerfully and disadvantageously upon individual local institutions.

The development of policy

FHE1 contained the gloomy statement that the development of policy in higher education was 'beyond the capacity either of government itself or of bodies such as the UGC or NAB' (as they then were). Sadly this remains the situation. Individual institutions frequently argue that they feel themselves to be operating in a context where there is no nationally agreed single policy which coherently addresses the needs of higher education. If this is so, is there a case for a national body, perhaps an amalgam of the higher education interests of the Policy Studies Institute (PSI), the Centre for Policy Studies (CPS) and the Council for Industry in Higher Education (CIHE), together with the Committee of Directors and Principals (CDP) and CVCP to give a national focus and to seek ways of reflecting regionally and thus through local institutions a coherent policy framework? There is a problem here, most apparent nationally but also with its regional and local reflections, and that is the apparent hostility to much of the research *within* universities and the apparent anathema to independent research about the business and function of higher education *itself*. This caution, indeed this resistance, must be addressed and confronted, as it refers to an area of prime market research which will and should affect the policy development of individual institutions.

In considering progress on these six key areas emerging from FHE1 a number of lateral themes emerge:

1 *Lay/community participation in academic decision making*
Most institutions of higher education now have some lay participation at their council or governing body level. There are some who do not. However, even when this is in place, is it sufficient? Is it indeed proper? Should there not be a more widespread debate which examines the arguments for and against a more intimate lay involvement, for example at faculty board level? The arguments here are in many cases delicate and highly charged. None the less to give a local community or indeed any community a sense of ownership of an institution of higher education in its midst, which is still supported to a large extent on the basis of proceeds from a fiscal levy, is not an unreasonable objective.

2 *New technologies*
Secondly, the application of new technologies in the broadest sense to institutional objectives merits consideration. Here there are at least two questions. First, are institutional management structures sufficiently numerate themselves to manage and implement new technologies as a part of their own process of growth? Secondly, is sufficient management encouragement and practical support by way of funding given within institutions to bring new technologies into play, for example in mixed mode teaching? Why is it that the mixture of modes which are potentially available, as between the Open University and other institutions of higher education, are not routinely in place? Where they exist they appear to rely, if not on chance, at best on one-off idiosyncratic arrangements.

3 *Marketing*
The emergence of marketing as an issue reflects both a more sophisticated public and the artificial engendering of a market situation in which institutions have been *de facto* compelled to compete with each other, sometimes not on a very efficient basis. There are significant implications here, from the design of product (course, set of services or other offering) to promoting these

offerings to specific or general audiences. Increasingly in a competitive market place institutions are having to ask themselves whether they have the appropriate professional skills within their own hierarchy; can they be developed from within or must they be recruited from without? Where the latter is the case, there is a generation of new professionals growing up within higher education which itself requires management of a kind that has sufficient professional awareness of the criteria within which marketing people operate.

4 *Management of research*

The management of research cannot be decoupled from the management of teaching and the management of contributions to continuing education. It raises issues related to the freedom of academic staff to continue to undertake research/consultancy in their own right without necessarily assuring some payback to the institution, and to deploy the rights associated with their intellectual property for their own purposes as opposed to the purposes of the institution who pays their salary. It is therefore a reasonable strategic question to ask how far is it appropriate for the management of research to be fully integrated into the corporate plan of any HE institution and to what extent does research have a 'life of its own' either for the individual or for the institutional departments.

5 *Transbinary mechanisms*

A fifth area of concern is the way in which any 'transbinary' mechanisms in the old sense of that term would or should operate at an institutional and regional level. We noted earlier the blurring of the boundary between advanced further education and higher education. However, at an institutional and regional level should the move towards transbinary provision and coherent planning of further and higher education on a regional basis be left to chance? Should it be left to the relatively random though financially effective workings of PICKUP-funded consortia? Or should there be more detailed codes worked out between government departments centrally and reflected in formal structures regionally and locally, which move us towards a genuine basis for planning of the total higher education provision in a region or at an institutional level?

6 *Management issues*

There is a significant amount to be learned from the ways in which styles of management have developed within individual universities and more corporately within the polytechnics since FHE1. Arguably there has been a move towards a more managerial style in university vice-chancelloreates, following the Jarratt Report (CVCP 1985). Is this apparent narrowing of the difference between UFC and PCFC institutions significant? Is it something that should be monitored and what are the lessons to be learned from it? In this general management context how best is the specific management of reward/incentive schemes to be approached from the viewpoint of individual institutions but still in the context of nationally agreed salary scales and national union negotiations? How can exceptional performance revealed locally be locally acknowledged? How best is the 'us' versus the 'them' of workers and management honestly and openly addressed in a 'self-governing academic community'?

7 *Central control and local government*
Finally there are two linked issues to be addressed at a local and institutional level. The first is how the tension between less central funding but relatively more central control of both policy and curriculum is to be handled at institutional level. This issue obviously impinges both upon individual institutional autonomies in an academic sense and also the extent to which individual institutions of higher education will or will not be willing to implement any nationally devised curriculum or set of standards (such as those in the higher levels of the national and vocational qualification system) which may affect institutions of higher education nationally. Second is the manifestation of co-operation or otherwise between government departments at local level. The Treasury already has concerns about the reporting lines of the TECs, which disburse substantial fractions of public money at a local level and whose lines of accountability are not wholly clear. Linked with that issue has to be the increasing input of public moneys into higher education from departments of government other than the DES and the nature of the management of that both nationally and institutionally.

The shape of many individual institutions has changed almost beyond recognition since FHE1. Some of the changes undoubtedly derive from that exercise; others are less planned, and in a context of continuing turbulence it is unlikely that we have reached a stability in the number and variety of life-forms within the higher education system.

Note

1. See Annex 1 to preceding chapter for details.

8

Governance: An Overview

Michael Shattock

Institutional level

At FHE2, the discussion of institutional governance and management concentrated on four questions. The first was about effectiveness. Is a democratic or participative approach more effective than the managerial style favoured by the Jarratt Report? Does extensive devolution of financial responsibility to departments assist or hinder effective management? Do we need more training for leadership and for governance? A second question relates to the value of setting objectives. There seems to be general agreement that the preparation of institutional plans and mission statements assists management and gives governing bodies a more strategic role. A further question has been about corporate loyalty. We hear a good deal about academics' loyalty to their subject and discipline and also to their students and to their department. Such loyalties are separate from and often seem to be in conflict with loyalty to their institution. This suggests that creating an effective organizational culture in institutions of higher education is a much higher priority than most people think. The last major question is the balance to be struck between competitiveness and collaboration, both within and between institutions. Personally I have no difficulty in accepting a competitive environment, but we should not forget the benefits of collaboration.

Let me draw some conclusions from the discussion. It is a truism to say that this is a time of great change and adjustment for institutions in higher education; polytechnics are taking on new responsibilities; universities are being forced to change. There are problems of size, of managerial experience, of authority and of capacity to change. I recall from FHE1 the quotation from Kenneth Durham, Chairman of Unilever, who said in 1983:

> I gain the impression that our higher educational institutions have neither the organizational structures nor as yet the management skills

to deal with what will be a difficult situation over the next few years. Industrialists have learned how to manage change in difficult times and I hope the need for academics to do the same will be an important lesson from our seminar.

I disagreed with that statement in 1983 and I disagree with it now. Institutions are learning, and the record over the last decade shows only three possible near market failures: Cardiff, Aberdeen and Dartington Hall. We have not actually had large scale institutional failures, and we have less to be ashamed of than we sometimes think in comparison to our commercial and business colleagues where market failures caused by lack of foresight, lack of financial control or just plain lack of common sense seem to be only too frequent. However that should not encourage complacency: we face a very testing time, with more students, less funding, and all the dangers of considerable over-extension. Perhaps our real test will come not from market failure which the government seems pledged to prevent, but from a degradation of our academic standing, a consistent move down-market.

The moral is that higher education institutions and the Funding Councils need to talk to one another a good deal more. At the moment I suspect that about 250 institutions of higher education are considering how they can fund additional student residences. This is ridiculous. The purchasing power of higher education should be sufficient to enable us to approach financial institutions and come up with a well worked out package, but we tend to be unhappy about collaborating on such issues. In this we perhaps resemble much of British industry which is also not very good at collaboration. I have nothing against management consultants but higher education needs to clear up its own messes, with more interaction and collaboration on questions of institutional management. One firm conclusion is that the two Funding Councils ought to think seriously about setting up some kind of task force to look at questions of institutional finance and management.

System level[1]

One line of argument produces some fairly radical conclusions: the binary system of the two Funding Councils should go and higher education, along with the crucial sector of further education, ought to be funded directly from government, along the lines of the Australian or the Dutch systems. There should be some sort of advisory body to the DES, and research funding should be passed over to the Advisory Board for Research Councils (ABRC).

Personally I disagree. I believe it would not be at all wise to have a system which did not have some way of differentiating institutions. The problem is that the binary line is too hard, too impermeable and is probably drawn in the wrong place. There are, one suspects, a number of university institutions that might sit more happily on the other side of the binary line. There may be some public sector institutions that would be more suited on the university side. But there is a lot to be said for a kind of Californian system, where the students move but the institutions are, as it were, stationary.

I am quite opposed to institutions being funded direct from the DES. This goes very much against the British tradition which has always distanced government from the direct funding of universities. I fear that it would only be a very short time before the accusation was made that ideology was involved in funding policies. Once that accusation was made relations between government and institutions would be irrevocably tainted. Handing research funding over to ABRC – an institution which is itself in some flux – would be a constraining rather than a liberating move. The ABRC has neither the machinery nor the breadth of subject interests to take on such a role.

I come back to the question of the need for more collaboration between UFC and PCFC. The two Councils will need to think about regional policy; about the provision of scientific manpower; about teacher training; about staffing the NHS and about collaboration with Europe. The two Funding Councils are better placed to discuss these fruitfully than the DES on its own. That is not to remove the DES from the scene but to say that there needs to be a dialogue between the Councils as independent bodies rather than one that is conducted entirely on DES terms. Naturally the DES will need to become involved.

It is worth stressing that as part of regional policy we need to focus on the further education sector. We do not need to invent community colleges or to ape America in this, but further education has a major place in the higher education system.

On the question of higher education policy studies, we would be wise not to tie up the whole future of higher education policy in one particular centre. There is major scope now for thinking more about higher education policy both within the UFC/PCFC Bristol office and in academic centres; the Economic and Social Research Council ought to think more about funding in this area. We would benefit from a multiplicity of studies of higher education policy rather than trying to concentrate it in one place.

My last thought is on the question of market and competitiveness *vis à vis* collaboration. One has to look back to FHE1 and conclude that we have benefited from market forces. They have released innovation, but we need balances. One of the strengths of the higher education system is the diversity of institutions, but leaving things entirely to market forces may lead to results which we might not like. We could find that the free play of the market might reduce diversity and encourage moving to a more homogeneous model. We might again find that real commercial attitudes could intrude. How would we feel about Leeds University taking over Leeds Polytechnic, or Manchester Polytechnic taking over Manchester University? It is important that we maintain the current diversity of institutions as well as the diversity of the system. That seems to me to argue against arbitrarily getting rid of the Funding Councils so recently set up and moving immediately to some new structure. We are in a long transitional phase which might extend over a whole decade, as the present changes take time to work through. We need therefore to get back to the question of thinking about the management of the system, and the management of the institutions in the context of a very complicated period of change, the outcomes of which it is not possible at present to forecast. Good management in a rapidly changing environment needs luck as well as leadership, and neither are in as much evidence as they need to be if a successful system of higher education is to emerge.

Note

1. See Chapter 1, note 4.

9

The Future and Further Education

Colin Flint

Introduction

As one of the speakers at FHE2 remarked, the acronym is understood by many people to refer not to 'The Future of Higher Education' but to 'further and higher education'. It was a pertinent point. The embracing of one definition by the other is perhaps the real subject.

At the time of FHE1, I was working, as a Principal, in the further education system. I have to confess that I was totally unaware that it had taken place, and I am reasonably confident that those involved spent little or no time on the part that FE had to play in the future of the nation's higher education system. The preoccupations centred on a falling participation rate – lower in 1980 than in 1970 – and on the consequence of a falling population of school leavers, both factors which might have turned the attention of at least some of the participants towards the further education colleges. But, as Gareth Williams has noted, 'the basic assumptions of the Robbins era were still in place. Expected demand from qualified school-leavers . . . was the mainspring of higher education planning' (see Chapter 2). There is little indication that the FE colleges were seen as an important element in the equation, either as supplier of students or as agents of change.

There has been, therefore, at least some movement. FE *was* present at FHE2, and an FE perspective on the future is seen as a proper part of this volume. More important, real progress is being made in several areas of the country towards articulated links between colleges and their neighbouring universities and polytechnics. There are very few colleges not now running programmes aimed at preparing adult students for entry into higher education: there can be no institution of higher education, whatever its age, tradition, or status, which is not now taking students who have come through the route which we provide. The announcement in April 1991 that the Colleges of FE are to be taken out of local authority control must also be cautiously welcomed. This can be made into the opportunity to create the policy for post-compulsory education that we have never had.

So what has changed? At its simplest and starkest, it is the recognition amongst most observers that Britain is facing a crisis, and that its education system is at the heart of the problems. As Sir Claus Moser and many others have noted, Britain is in danger of becoming the least adequately educated of all advanced nations. The fact that the participation rate for sixteen-to-eighteen-year-olds in full-time education in Britain is so low must give us serious pause: in fact, our rate is significantly lower than that of all our international competitors.

As a nation, we do not value education sufficiently highly. The majority of the British still regard it as something to stop doing at the earliest opportunity. The contrast is stark in the United States, in the Pacific Rim nations and in much of Europe. We are the only advanced nation still permitting sixteen-year-olds to go into work that carries no training entitlement. The waste is incalculable: for the vast majority it has been irreversible.

What we need is a change in the culture. We need systems that encourage participation, at all ages and all levels, and remove the obstacles that now litter the path. We need to set a new tone, and to redefine the goals and the objectives. We almost certainly need to be willing to sacrifice a few sacred cows. Our faith in the supremacy of GCE A level as the main means of separating those who can benefit from higher education from those who cannot is no longer defensible. The A level system is the biggest barrier to reform and the major cause of distortion in our system. It is unequivocally designed for the minority, yet is seen as the criterion of success or failure by the whole.

We need a system which will reward and value success, not limit by failure. Above all, we need to stop making the damaging and invalid distinctions between 'academic' and 'vocational' routes which are all too evident in the minds of education ministers, academics and too many parents. Even in our current crisis, we are in danger of preserving the mind-set which looks to *educating* those most capable of benefiting from education, and simply *training* the rest. It won't work. Higher education planned on this model has no future.

The purpose of this chapter is to direct attention towards some of the components of a better system.

The current scope of the FE system

The history of further education has been somewhat haphazard. Colleges developed for a variety of reasons, usually clearly related to local educational and industrial need. Part-time courses for employed people were – and are – a main element, initially through evening classes, later through day-release. The major components of your local college nowadays are likely to be:

- a range of full-time courses for young people with particular career objectives, and who want to stay in full-time education (but not remain in schools) whilst being offered a much wider choice of routes;

Table 1 Enrolments (000s) in further education, 1980–1990

	1980/81	*1985/86*	*1986/87*	*1987/88*	*1988/89*	*1989/90*
Full-time	296	340	347	354	359	377
Part-time	1158	1319	1384	1428	1559	1609
Totals	1454	1659	1731	1782	1918	1986

- full-time and part-time day courses for those returning to education after a break (to which a key contribution is usually disenchantment with their earlier educational experience). Numbers of such students have grown very rapidly in recent years, especially in various 'Access' programmes;
- part-time programmes for employed people, through day-release or evening study;
- programmes for unemployed people, mainly through involvement with government training schemes;
- community education courses covering a wide spectrum of demand, and offered usually as evening classes, but sometimes as summer school, Saturday morning classes and other day provision;
- short course provision for industry and commerce;
- open learning opportunities through 'Flexistudy' and other supported distance learning, and learning workshops.

This diversity is one of the reasons for the success of the colleges. They have grown very substantially and fairly consistently from the 1960s. The related needs of an expanding economy and the postwar bulge gave considerable impetus to the development of the full-time courses for school leavers, and the nature of most colleges was changed as a result. More recently, they have become the major providers of training for the unemployed, and they are by far the most important agency making provision for adult returners. It is important to emphasize that students from all of the different categories listed above can, and do, proceed on to higher education.

Education for all

What the FE system does, and can do to great effect if properly supported, is create the base for a mass system of post-compulsory education.

There has been a 24 per cent increase in the numbers of those over the age of twenty-five in our colleges in the last five years. The average age of the student body in FE has risen in every recent year, and, as Table 1 above shows, overall levels of participation have gone up despite the reductions in the numbers of school leavers since 1986.

Colleges have become better at matching provision to the needs of a different set of students, with good childcare facilities, advice and counselling services, courses and programmes planned with the needs of adult students in mind. We are active in the crucial area of accreditation of prior achievement and learning, so that we can enable students to start at the points suitable for them, not just take a predetermined course and starting point. The modularization of the curriculum, and the devising of a properly articulated credit and transfer system – both essential components of structures that will meet the needs of new students – are being put in place in the colleges. Fifteen successful years of work on BTEC programmes have been an excellent preparation.

Further education has demonstrably taken seriously its role as the major provider of a comprehensive post-school education service, delivered locally. The use of 'extension centres', or 'local learning centres' to support and encourage access to main college sites has been seen as an important part of the delivery; accessibility to the systems themselves has been very actively encouraged, and the philosophy of the colleges, certainly the most successful ones, has been one of open access.

There can surely be no argument that such provision is necessary, whatever the standpoint. It is just as important to improve education and training opportunities for adults of working age, whether or not in work, as it is to improve the participation rates of school leavers. Eighty per cent of the people who will be in the workforce ten years hence are already in the labour market. We have immense problems with this educational and training backlog, but we cannot afford to neglect it if we are to remain an advanced economy. We need a 'high skills equilibrium': to achieve it we will have to reach backwards to help the casualties of present and past systems as well as adopt new philosophies to underpin our structures for the future. It will require enormous commitment – from government, from industry, and from the education system. The role of the further education sector will be crucial.

Access

FE has been involved in 'Access' for nearly 20 years. It was probably Nelson & Colne College which was the real pioneer, with its splendid 'open college' initiatives with Lancaster University and Preston (now Lancashire) Polytechnic. These programmes eschewed O and A level, and were based on college-devised and HE-validated courses of study which were highly successful, both in attracting adult students and in securing progression. This scheme became the basis of the Lancashire Open College Federation, and such schemes are now in place in most areas of the country.

Access in this form has been largely about increasing participation from targeted groups, whether adults, or black students, or any other of the educationally disadvantaged. Most success has been achieved so far in increasing participation amongst women. In these schemes, special programmes of study become the main vehicle, and there are resource implications, such as in advisory and counselling services, in the writing of new materials, and the provision of childcare. The colleges of further education can claim conspicuous success for their part in the widespread development and acceptance of this work.

The other kind of 'access' is about increasing participation from the existing participating groups. There has been some success in this field too, especially in the polytechnics and colleges of higher education, where numbers have risen substantially in the last two years. There is clearly much more demand, and various reasons have been adduced for it, including the apparent success of GCSE, and greater affluence.

This is clearly to be welcomed, but there is a danger that success in the latter kind of access will make the former seem less important: if the 'traditional', school-leaving student intake continues to rise despite the demography, why bother? The answer is, of course, that we should be as concerned about those who missed out first-time round as about the present crop. If we wait for our educational attitudes to be changed by the effect of a larger number of graduates on society, then it will take a generation. We can't wait, and nor should we. Access, capital A, must remain a priority.

The scope of the colleges

It may help to show a sketch of a part of the further education service. Solihull College of Technology is larger than most, and no two colleges are wholly alike, but its profile is not untypical of the kind of scope that is to be found in most of the 400+ colleges in Britain (see Table 2). Those not familiar with the colleges may be struck by the range of curriculum, the diversity of modes of attendance, the age profile, and the numbers involved. The colleges are the only part of the British educational systems which is comprehensive, in the fullest sense, in terms of ability, age, aptitude and the ambitions we help to realize, and the only sector which responds to the needs of such a large and diverse proportion of the population. And, to labour the point, it is amongst this large admixture that we will find the 'new' students for higher education. Further education sees it as one of the primary tasks to bring people back into education. We are the *enabling* element in the post-compulsory system. We are the hinge on which the door, firmly shut for most, can be opened.

FE and HE: one system?

Even if we take a very wide definition of advanced education, so that it includes both further and higher sectors – and most in Britain would emphatically reject such a hypothesis – then this country has a participation rate of less than 35 per cent of the cohort at eighteen. Korea aims at 80 per cent by the end of the century: France at 75 per cent. In Britain there is a good deal of fudging around a target of doubling the participation in 25 years.

In order to achieve even this target, we would need to see:

Table 2 Solihull College of Technology (Academic Year 1989/90)

a) *Total enrolments*   17573   *Age profile of all students*
   Full-time   2383   16–19   4065
   Part-time day (released from employment)   1486   20–21   1856
                                                                       22–25   2891
   Part-time day (not released)   5407   26–35   2766
   Evening only   3722   36–45   2504
   Distance Learning   216   46–55   1608
   Short courses   4359   56+   1883

(Note: Figures *exclude* 2000 enrolments at Summer School but *include* Saturday community courses)

b) *Range of curriculum:*

Business and Technician (BTEC) National Diplomas in:
Business & Finance, Art & Design, Hotel & Catering, Design, Engineering, Engineering & Management, Graphic Design, Distribution, Care, Nursery Nursing, Leisure & Recreation, Travel & Tourism, Language & Overseas Trade, Fashion, Photography, Media, Science, Computing.

Business and Technician 1st level qualifications in:
Catering, Design, Engineering, Distribution, Business Studies, Leisure & Tourism, Science.

GCE A level programmes:
Health Studies, Science, Drama Studies, Communication, Media, English & Humanities, Social Science, Maths & Computing, Sports Studies, Pre-Teaching, 34 A level single subjects.

GCSE: 42 single subjects.

Professional qualifications:
Institute of Linguists, Institute of Bankers, Institute of Marketing, Supervisory Studies, Association of Accountancy Technicians, Association of Legal Secretaries, Association of Medical Secretaries, Practice Administrators & Receptionists, Confederation of Institutions of Beauty Therapy & Cosmetology, Institute of Administrative Managers, Institute of Legal Executives, Institute of Personnel Managers, Institute of Credit Management, Diploma RSA, Licentiate of City & Guilds of London Institute, Institute of Industrial Management, Chartered Institute of Secretaries, Association of Chartered and Certified Accountants.

Other technical & vocational qualifications:
Art & Design Foundation, Certificate in Pre-Vocational Education, Family and Community Care, Nursery Nursing, Hairdressing, Beauty Therapy, Floristry, General Engineering, Refrigeration Engineering, Hotel Receptionists, Secretarial Studies

Access programmes, and higher education affiliated courses

- much higher A level attainment rates;
- participation rates by women which match those of men;
- participation by mature students increasing by 50 per cent;
- participation by those qualifying through vocational routes matching the A level rate;
- much higher participation by social groups III–V.

In brief, we need to see three parallel and eventually equal routes into higher education:

a) eighteen- and nineteen-year-olds and qualified by A levels (or Scottish Highers);
b) eighteen- and nineteen-year-olds with vocational qualifications;
c) mature students, qualified as much by experience as by examination.

The RSA report, *More Means Different*, provides a most detailed and compelling account of the deficiencies of the current arrangements and the rationale for new philosophies. As its author, Sir Christopher Ball, says, '. . . it is conceptually wrong to treat as opposites terms such as education and training, academic and vocational, or even skills and knowledge. In each case these terms represent at most the two ends of a gradation.' (Ball 1990, Chapter Two). He adds, in another context but equally applicable, '. . . we need a new vocabulary to do justice to new concepts. Our existing language is the product of traditional patterns, and constrains our thinking.'

The language may indeed be changing. The political parties now vie with each other to seize the high ground in the post-sixteen debate. Kenneth Clarke takes the colleges out of LEA control; Jack Straw re-invents Higginson in his proposals for the reform of A levels; further education gets more exposure in the media than it has ever enjoyed before. Enough has now happened to ensure that significant change must follow.

New concepts and new thinking are slowly asserting themselves. We are now seeing the beginnings of a system of credit accumulation and transfer which must receive full recognition and value. It then needs to be applied. Having achieved a patchwork of open access federations covering large areas of the country, we need to make them into a network. What is required is a system which is genuinely nation-wide, and indeed international. The educational credits gained in Accrington must be recognized in Aberdeen and Aberystwyth (and, soon, in Aachen and Avignon) and known to be so by employers as well as by the gate-keepers of the higher education institutions. This in turn implies a nationally recognized validating body. The system would need to cover the full range of the curriculum. There is little point in creating a new structure which repeats the mistakes of the past: this is all about accrediting achievement, not establishing new pecking orders.

We need a system that recognizes the value of prior experience and of levels of competence. The key to the accreditation of prior learning (APL), or achievement, is in institutional validation and Britain will have to overcome its innate suspicion of such arrangements. There are no dangers in this: APL is a stepping stone, not a terminal qualification, and the colleges have substantial experience in educational assessment and counselling. The accreditation of prior learning, when established and recognized, will be one of the means by which the British educational system will be liberated.

Franchising and affiliation

The franchising concept, in which HE institutions licence FE colleges to do (usually) one year of a four-year degree, has now a number of examples; the '2 + 2' is a more challenging and ultimately much more fruitful way forward. In effect, this should lead to affiliated status for those colleges of FE which can demonstrate to the satisfaction of their HE partner, their capability to teach to the intermediate stage of a first degree. This would make Britain very similar indeed to the American model, the community colleges; and FE colleges would, through it, soon match the prestige and importance that their transatlantic counterparts enjoy. It is vital, however, that our planning should give high priority, and sympathetic help, to part-time routes. This could be the reform which produces most change of all. The universities and polytechnics need to give much more consideration to the needs of part-time students, in the way that FE does now, and government needs to find ways of encouraging and supporting them.

A recent report (from a minister in the Department of Education and Science) said that student loans for part-time students may be possible when there is sufficient cash from repayment of loans by existing students. It was calculated that this may be by the year 2006. This was one of the more fatuous of recent comments about the future of higher education in Britain. There have been many others. These are fundamental misunderstandings about the nature of a mass system of higher education and what its characteristics will need to be. Though we clearly have to start from where we are, we cannot achieve what must be achieved by placing our faith in, simply, more of what we have always had. We need not only a new vocabulary, but also a new philosophy, new strategies.

There are some major problems to be overcome. Whilst there is much convergent talk these days, there is an equal amount of divergent action. Most people have welcomed the Training and Enterprise Councils; but their funding has been cut before they come into operation. Ministers talk of the importance of vocational education; A levels, however, are to be protected at all costs. Colleges eagerly co-operate in the development of new degree programmes; but neither UFC nor PCFC can fund our part of them. The contribution of the FE colleges to a better co-ordinated and more rational system of post-sixteen education and training has never been more necessary. FE is now in some respects the most vulnerable element of the whole state system, unable to threaten to opt out, not even statutory, and at the mercy of councils desperate to reduce the level of their local tax, whatever form that may take.

There are major challenges here too for the FE colleges. We cannot pretend that we have offered a uniformly good service; if we had, then perhaps our role would have achieved more recognition earlier. There have been widely differing ambitions and purposes amongst those responsible for the colleges and we have to admit to some variable quality, and an inability on occasion to respond to new needs. Some of the colleges at one time deserved a reputation for poor levels of pastoral care, for inadequate advice and guidance services, and for inflexibility over modes and times of delivery.

However, there is considerable evidence now to support the claims that there has been very substantial progress in the last ten years. Much educational innovation has started or been nurtured in the FE system: open learning, and flexible delivery systems, Access courses, pre-vocational education, integrated academic and vocational provision. The numbers using our service are corroboration of our levels of quality. The good colleges have developed their own space in the system: they are providing a breadth of service to students, to industry, and to the community which no other sector can match.

These good FE colleges in Britain demonstrate, every day, their faith in the capacities of people to achieve more: more than they thought they could, more than has been expected of them, more than their previous educational experience had allowed them to see. That is why the colleges are an important part of the systems we must have for the future, and why they must be supported in their efforts to provide them.

10

Quality in Higher Education

Pauline Perry

In the early 1980s, when people spoke of quality in higher education, they spoke of it in rather lofty and abstract terms. This was not because of any inability to define it, but because there was a high level of consensus in the country, and perhaps throughout Europe, about the issue of academic quality. There was also an assumption (in retrospect, perhaps more dangerous) that some universities throughout the world were in themselves the benchmark of quality, against which all other institutions could be measured without any further defining of the ingredients of quality, or indeed the criteria by which this perceived quality had been achieved.

In the 1990s, the issues concerning quality have greatly changed. Quality is no longer seen as a philosophical concept; it is now being defined and measured, largely by those who fund the system rather than by those within it, and within their definitions and criteria it is being rewarded (or its absence punished), in terms of hard cash.

High quality ratings in research determine substantial parts of the budget of universities, while the HMI quality ratings of teaching and learning in the polytechnics determine the price we are paid for educating our students, as well as the number of students we are encouraged to recruit. Those in the system who now cry at this pain, might well reflect that the early signs of what was to come were already apparent at the beginning of the 1980s. I ask myself now whether we within the educational system worked hard enough ourselves to define, measure and above all explain to those outside what we were doing, and what criteria we believed were appropriate for the definitions of quality. With the wisdom of hindsight, how sensible it would have been to demonstrate our ability to make hard-edged judgements at our own institutional level, rather than armchair statements about the impossibility of making such judgements.

The idea of quality is after all as much an industrial concept as it is an academic one. The nineteenth-century founder of Lucas Industries, Joseph Lucas, once said, 'Quality is remembered long after price is forgotten'. He knew, as any shopper in the high street knows, that the standard of quality we expect is related to the price we are prepared to pay. No one expects to get a Rolls Royce engine for the price of a Honda Civic, and yet as customers we understand well what we mean by quality at different price levels. Strangely, and I think sadly, this is a debate which the universities and polytechnics have yet to undertake with their funding councils. The urgency of clarifying that particular issue is becoming more apparent each year, as the amount of money per student is driven downwards, and institutions adjust in various ways to reflect that fact. We must be open about the different standards of quality we are offering at changing price levels.

Defining quality

Given the weight, in financial and marketing terms, which is now put on quality judgements, it should be that the definitions of quality are more clear. To a considerable extent, there is now more general agreement on the elements which together make up a judgement about quality in higher education, and this agreement has in itself been an ingredient in improving quality. There is now almost universal acceptance of two major principles: firstly, that research activity is a necessary part of the equation of quality judgement of either an institution as a whole or an individual department; secondly, that the quality of teaching as experienced by the student is an important ingredient in the judgement. Although to the lay outsider these principles might seem unremarkable, agreement on these two issues has by no means been easily reached.

The link between research and teaching, as two of the ingredients in judgements of quality in higher education, must take us back to the preliminary question of what is perceived as the purpose of the higher education system, for it is against those purposes that the success or failure of any individual institution must be judged. In this complex activity, the simple judgement of the students about their experience, although a vital ingredient, is not itself sufficient evidence. The higher education system, uniquely in the commercial world, must see its students both as its customers and as its product. Our students must be attracted into our institutions, by the courses we offer, the accommodation and personal care we give them, the excellence of our teaching, our location, the friends they can make, the leisure activities they can undertake, and the attractions of the campus. All institutions invest money and skill in presenting these elements in the best way that we can, in order to attract our potential customer – the student – to come to us, bringing with her the fees and resourcing which attach to a student via the public purse, and in some cases via private sources also.

But two, three or four years later, these students become the product we must sell to the potential employers outside. No matter how much they have enjoyed their course and their time with us, we will have failed both them and the larger community which supports us financially and morally, if we have produced graduates and diplomates who are incapable of earning their own living, or of contributing to the economy and adult society in which they live.

At the widest level of course, the aims of students and the community outside are not necessarily in conflict, since there can be few students who come to us for the crucial years of their lives which they spend in higher education, without some expectation that they will both enjoy their study and enhance their life chances by the award they receive. Nevertheless, at the day to day level, there is a real tension between the demands and choices which students make, against the demands and expectations of society outside. Until very recently, few students in the Humanities welcomed the offering of information technology as a required part of their course: neither did students of engineering welcome the inclusion of a European language as a compulsory element in their study. Nevertheless, to meet the demands of employers, and the legitimate expectations of society, it is vital that these elements form part of the knowledge and skills with which Humanities graduates or engineers emerge into the adult working world.

Resolving these tensions is a challenge for the secondary schools, for parents and for employers, none of whom perhaps make the message of society's needs as clear to young people as is necessary, if they are to understand the effect of the choices they make.

Perhaps we might resolve the conflict, or apparent conflict, of definition of purpose, by agreeing that overall the purposes of higher education are to meet the needs of its students in the widest possible sense, including their personal, academic and learning needs, as well as their long term need to find fulfilment in contributing to their society. In order to do this, institutions must not only offer the attractions which might ensnare the student at the point of choice, but must further ensure that their courses provide the range of knowledge and skills which will be appropriate for the foreseeable future of the society outside education, not only in the narrow economic sense but in the wider sense of society's aspirations for itself. Even to begin to fill such a remit is an awesome task. To fulfil it well, to deliver the much sought-after 'quality' which we seek, implies staff who are themselves tuned to the best of society's aspirations for itself, both in human and in intellectual terms. This means not only should the teaching be informed by appropriate research, whether practical and applied in the polytechnics, or 'blue sky' and pure in the better universities; but also that those who teach should be in tune with the industrial, commercial and cultural excellence in practice which is to be found in the world outside. As John Ruskin once wrote, 'Quality is never an accident; it is always the result of intelligent effort'. Higher education institutions must make overt and conscious the intelligent effort they devote to the achievement of quality in what they do.

As I have already indicated, I believe that the definition of quality is not absolute. The diversity of institutions within higher education seems to me right, proper, and an important facet of the richness of the provision of higher education in most modern western societies. The concept of 'fitness for purpose' is therefore an important one, in forming any judgement of quality. Fitness for purpose is of course only a threshold judgement: all of us hope to go beyond that. Nevertheless, a clear definition, and an honest one, of the differing purposes of different institutions, and the consequent appropriateness of quality judgements, seems to me to be one part of the dialogue which has not yet been properly exposed. Not every singer can be a soloist, nor would we wish a musical world in which this was so. Some training is designed to produce the concert performer, the solo virtuoso, while the rest (and the majority) is designed to produce the well-tuned members of the choir, or the good team members of the orchestra. It would be dishonest of higher education institutions to pretend that all of us were in the business of producing the solo concert performer; equally dishonest of those who judge us, to judge the good training school for the orchestra members, against the standard of the international conservertoire which trains only solo performers of world repute. The challenge of course is largely to those of us within institutions, whether senior managers or those who plan, design and teach the courses, to understand clearly our purpose and mission, and to ensure that what we do is appropriate to and serves the fulfilment of that purpose.

Judging teaching

Nevertheless, throughout higher education across the UK, judgements of quality are being made by those outside our institutions, in ways which bear very much on our own ability to fulfil our purposes, and the aspirations we have for ourselves. Judgements about research quality have now almost a decade of history behind them in the universities, and if direct money for research is given to the polytechnics, similar judgements will be applied there. Judgements have been made largely on the grounds of the volume of research output, together with elements such as reference citations, and ability to attract external funding, which broadly represent the validation by peers of the quality of the volume. There are of course difficult issues in the relationship between quality and volume (*Gone with the Wind* was, after all, its author's only book, and she might therefore fare very badly on the volume judgement; but there are few who would claim that her single book was a failure!). Despite these problems, most academics seem content to accept the rough and ready approach, which the years have already refined.

Judgements of teaching quality are less easily made, but nevertheless many attempts are now being made, both by the setting up of the universities' Academic Audit Unit, and by the measures suggested by the Polytechnics and Colleges Funding Council's Committee on Teaching Quality. The longest track record in this field belongs to Her Majesty's Inspectors, who have been making such judgements for many decades, and indeed publishing them (for the public sector in all aspects of higher education, and for the universities in respect of teacher education), in increasing volume over the past few years. It is their judgements of teaching quality, and the quality of student achievement, which as we have noted now contribute to the

PCFC's decisions about the number of places and their price in individual institutions. Nevertheless, hard-working though they are, and ubiquitous though they may seem to polytechnic directors, HMI can make judgements on only a very tiny proportion of the millions of hours of teaching that take place each year in the polytechnic sector alone. So far, they are the only body of people either inside or outside institutions who systematically observe the teaching and learning process in classroom, laboratory or workshop, and who place great weight on this observation in formulating judgements of the overall quality of a course or department. They will of course formulate the overall judgement on a wider range of factors than their classroom observation alone, including the response of students to the teaching environment; the nature of that environment itself, and its relationship with the outside world; the background of research and scholarly activity; and the care in curriculum and syllabus construction which staff have put into the course both in its initial stages, and in practice as experienced by the students.

The polytechnics, accredited by the Council for National Academic Awards (CNAA), continue to put a heavy emphasis on the initial validation of a course, and the regular review of that course every three to five years, based on monitoring statistics, external examiners' reports and the representations of students. The PCFC teaching quality committee has followed a similar line, although it has made a most important step forward from the CNAA criteria, in that it has suggested that all institutions should give account of the internal measures they have instituted to ensure that the quality of teaching and learning is maintained and enhanced. Also, most crucially, they have recommended that the appraisal of teaching staff should include appraisal of their performance in their teaching role.

If this latter criterion were to be applied with rigour, then the judgements of teaching quality would go beyond the checklists of systems and procedures which institutions have put in train in order to enhance the quality of teaching, and would provide evidence about the quality of teaching performance as experienced by students. Heads of department and other senior staff in institutions are, however, both reluctant and as yet inexperienced, in making quality judgements about the quality of teaching. In spite of the teaching quality committee's recommendations, and union agreement to the concept of appraisal, there is still considerable resistance on the part of lecturers to being observed in their classrooms.

I do however have a more fundamental and philosophical difficulty with the checklists of input data which appear to be used to make up the judgements about teaching quality. It seems wholly logical to suggest that the necessary conditions for quality include the performance of the teachers; the construction of the course; the devices put in train by the institution to enhance the quality of lecturers' performance; the necessary links with industry; the existence of appropriate accommodation, furniture and equipment for teaching; as well as the backup of good library and learning resource facilities. This list however provides only the necessary, not the sufficient condition for a judgement of quality to be made. Quality in teaching in higher education equals first and foremost, I would argue, the quality of the students' achievement at the end of their course. What a student knows, understands and is able to do is the chief and legitimate object of the measurement of teaching quality. Such measurements are made by the examiners, including the external examiners on whose shoulders sharpened responsibilities now lie.

Assuming that we trust, as we must, the examination assessment systems throughout higher education in the UK, with their many cross-checks and external controls, we must surely accept that the measured achievement of the student at the point of receiving her or his final award, is, or ought to be, an almost wholly sufficient measure of the quality of the course. I say almost, because I shall argue that there is one more element which needs to be taken into account. It would, however, be a logical absurdity to make a judgement that 'the students achieved high marks, and performed very successfully, but this was a course where the teaching is very unsuccessful.' Can the students succeed if their lecturers do not? Or conversely, can the lecturers be counted successful if their students are not? Those who advocate judgements based on institutional strategies for success, rather than success itself, may be in danger of such illogicality. What the customers demand and expect of higher education, to return to our original analysis, must surely begin with an expectation of achievement in the courses which is the best of which they as individuals are capable of achieving, and the best achievement that their future employers and colleagues have a right to expect. This does imply that the judgement of quality should begin with an analysis of student achievement, which in turn is balanced against the nature of the intake. I would not, however, argue that one should 'make allowances' for an intake which included mature students with unconventional qualifications – neither they nor their institutions would wish this. Some additional merit must accrue to institutions and to students who move a further distance from attainment at the beginning of the course to attainment at the end, but it is fair and right that achievements at the end of the course should no longer be weighted for the nature of the intake.

A fair judgement would have to go further than looking at the examination results alone. We should look beyond the students' success to the quality of their experience on their course. It would not be enough to say that the end result was good, if the experience of the students was so poor that they had to work twice as hard, and struggle twice as much, against the inadequate. The total resourcing of learning – the environment; the accommodation; the books and other equipment; the quality of the lecturers and their availability to students for academic counselling and assistance; the design and pace of the course are all quite legitimate objects of a quality judgement.

So it would be quite logical to make a statement about a course which said, 'This is a very successful course, on which students perform very well, but the facilities available for the course, and the environment in which it takes place, are very poor.' Indeed, this is the only kind of statement which could legitimately be made about a course where the results were good, but where we wished to judge the totality of the course as of less than high quality. Alternatively, one might well be making a judgement about the nature of the assessment itself. Many of us in higher education are less than happy about some of the professional examinations which our students are required to pass. 'Success' on such a course might well be the best that we could give, although neither we (nor in many cases our students) would consider the course itself a satisfactory experience. Here again, these circumstances should temper the judgements which are made, with common sense and an understanding of reality. HMI, the Academic Audit Unit, the CNAA and others could well join with us in higher education to bring pressure to bear on the professional bodies whose requirements force students into a narrow and irrelevant straightjacket in their training experience.

A further reservation would also have to be registered, before we were satisfied that the course where all final year students achieved high results in their examination was necessarily a 'good' course. It would be important to look at the early failure and drop-out rate which achieved such good results. Many of our academic colleagues in the US will admit to the disincentives of the system in many universities for giving weak students the benefit of the doubt in the early stages of their course. Where the measurement of their own teaching performance is made against the success of their final year students, it is clearly to their interest to ensure that only those sure of succeeding remain at the final hurdle. The criteria for measurement all too quickly become the message of the meaning and purpose of an activity, and it behoves all involved in the assessment of academic teaching effort in higher education to ensure that the messages conveyed are those which will benefit all our customers and their needs.

Quality and resource allocation

Where the judgement made is of high student performance, with all the caveats I have suggested, despite a poor environment and poor facilities, a very real problem is posed for those who use such judgements to determine our levels of funding. It would seem hard to defend a decision to take resources away from a course where students achieved obvious success, and yet where HMI or others have commented that despite the student success the level of facilities is so poor that student experience is impoverished: but the funding council might well, in present circumstances, remove any additional students or funding from that course or area of activity.

Of course, there are nil-cost steps which can be taken to improve learning experience, within the framework of a course which is otherwise successful. These should be encouraged at all levels; by HMI (as they do), by the funding councils, as well as by the management of the university or polytechnic itself. This is where those systems put in train to enhance the quality of teaching and learning are important and it is right for the funding councils to ask questions about whether these systems are in place. A well designed course, taught by people who have been given the maximum support by the institution, and who, where possible, have been chosen because they demonstrated skill in teaching, can however only be judged of high quality if it is also effective in producing high achievement on the part of the students who follow it. Both aspects, therefore, the output and the support systems, should be equal parts of the judgement, and the hard-edged funding decisions which are made.

Resourcing and Management

My logistic problems, however, arise when the level of resourcing is added to the equation of a quality judgement. I have no difficulty with the inclusion of resources in the judgement of quality as an abstract concept, but at the practical level of decisions about funding, it seems neither just nor logical to say, 'Students do well on this course, the course is well designed, and the institution has done everything in its power to ensure that those who teach on it are appropriately qualified and skilled. However, the level of accommodation and resources is so poor that we believe we should take further resources away from this course in future.'

I would not wish to argue that the level of resourcing is not closely linked to a judgement of ideal quality. I would, however, argue that within the necessarily limited resources which the country has for the expansion of higher education in the next decade and beyond, the defensible indices of quality used for funding purposes should rest firstly, on the outward measures of student achievement, including their acceptability by employers; and secondly, on the institutional measures taken to ensure that the maximum use is made of the limited resources available. This of course leads inexorably to judgements of the efficiency of the management and administration of the institution. The deployment of resources, the decisions about use of staff time, the setting of appropriate goals and targets, all properly belong to management and are a reflection of its quality. Indeed, the creation of a climate in which professionals may perform at their own maximum level with students is the prime task of managers at all levels throughout the higher education system. Judgements of quality therefore cannot exclude the quality of departmental heads, deans, directorate or vice-chancellorate.

The freedom of manoeuvre for management at any level is, however, not infinite. The total level of resourcing is to a large extent outside the control of either the institutions or the funding councils. While I believe the system has still some room to manoeuvre in the staff–student ratio, and wise and careful decisions will have to be made about the appropriate teaching styles for different students at different stages of their undergraduate and postgraduate learning, it is unlikely that there are many higher education institutions where economies in the academic staff budget can be achieved at a level where the massive problems of accommodation can be wholly solved. Many of us inherited from the local authorities buildings which were poorly maintained and inappropriate to the task of modern high technology education. Indeed, many of them are ill-fitted and expensive to adapt to the changing teaching styles which would be necessary to effect the very economies we are seeking. These are problems which our outside masters must share with us, rather than dismissing them as entirely a matter for internal management to resolve. I am not one of those who argues that every institution should have laboratories as well equipped as the Cavendish in Cambridge; chapels as magnificent as Kings College Chapel; lawns as green and well tended as the Backs along the Cam; nor that all students should have available to them the libraries of college, faculty and university on offer for the Cambridge undergraduate, together with the weekly supervision and the senior tutor or counsel. Diversity implies inequality, in higher education as in all aspects of life. But it is important to be honest about these differences, and to agree that judgements which are made are made in the light of known realities of such differences, not on some ideal beyond the capacity of the nation or the individual institution to achieve.

The last decade has seen, for all of us, a clarification of our own awareness of quality issues and a sharpening of management decisions which bear upon them. I hope above all the decade will be remembered as one where those who work in higher education became clearer about their mission, less concerned to strive for equality throughout the system, but to strive for achievement of goals and fulfilment of mission, appropriate to the diverse and varied system which we have.

11

Quality and Qualities: An Overview

Christopher Ball

Introduction

I was a signatory of FHE1. The publication of the eleven volumes of the study in 1981–83 almost exactly coincided with the creation of the National Advisory Body for Local Authority (later Public Sector) Higher Education (1982–88), which I chaired. The agenda, the analysis and the recommendations of FHE1 continuously informed the work of NAB during its lifetime and are still relevant and influential today.

One of the first decisions of the Board of NAB was to hold a residential weekend to discuss what seemed to us the three most difficult issues facing us. It is interesting to compare them with the themes chosen for FHE2. Some issues seemed relatively straightforward in those days – at least, they seemed so to an inexperienced and brashly confident planning body. Governance did not detain us. We thought we knew how to manage a system of higher education. Access was the primary task: we believed we knew how to go about it. The expansion of the system of public sector higher education through the 1980s is some measure of the success of that enterprise. The three problem areas were the regional dimension, the role of research, and quality.

Since 1982 I perceive a shift in thinking about the regional issue from concern about the role of local authorities towards the view that it is the local responsibility of institutions of higher education that is important. There are probably too many universities, polytechnics and even colleges aspiring to a national (or international) role; too few local or regional institutions. After 1992 it will be Brussels, rather than Westminster, that takes the lead in making arrangements for education and training for those above the age of sixteen. Brussels interacts best with regional bodies, not national ones. The issue for the UK is how to develop an effective regional structure in England to match the natural regions of Scotland, Wales and Northern Ireland. Time is short.

As far as *research* is concerned, this is and always has been mainly a university responsibility and a university problem. There are two keys to the future. First, we must learn to make the distinction between (fundamental) research and scholarship, the latter of which is a necessary adjunct to good teaching, the former of which is not. Secondly we must be brave enough to transfer basic research funds from the UFC to the Research Councils, creating single stream research funding, distributed thereafter in open competition to all institutions on merit. There would of course have to be transitional arrangements. The answers are known; it is political will and courage that is lacking.

Quality is more difficult. There is a preliminary question: what exactly is 'quality'? The absence of an adequate language for talking about it indicates the lack of a clear concept behind that magic word. Looking back at FHE1 I see that we called for 'a reliable quality assurance mechanism'. At that stage CNAA was deemed adequate for the polytechnic and college sector; we therefore recommended that the universities should establish an academic review body which should collaborate with the CNAA. The judgement we have to make today is whether the current arrangements can in fact be correctly described as reliable.

The CNAA has transformed itself, and its relationship with institutions, with the development of accreditation. The Vice-Chancellors and Principals have set up for the universities an Academic Audit Unit, whose character has been described by its Director as rigorous, sceptical, independent and credible. Much progress has been made since 1983. It is perhaps the clearest example of the FHE1 recommendations being acted upon. That is what we wanted to see, and it has happened. But we are left with some questions in our minds. The first is the apparent exclusion from the Audit Unit of a polytechnic contribution. Can there be real collaboration with the CNAA if polytechnic and college members are excluded? I doubt it. Secondly, there is something of a compromise over the publication of the audit results. The Director tells us that: "The unit will have no regulatory powers and universities will be free to publish or withhold their reports". At this stage I remain unconvinced that the new arrangements will prove reliable, but they could become so. There is a flavour, familiar to me from many similar occasions over the last ten years, of the universities doing the minimum in order to avoid trouble, rather than taking possession of the new agenda and making the running. The leadership of the universities in higher education is sadly missed.

A model for the discussion of quality

In order to talk about quality we need a model (see Figure 1). The key features of the model are, first, the various plural nouns in place of the usual singulars. We are starting to talk about qualities rather than quality. Qualities need a variety of definitions; those definitions will relate to a variety of

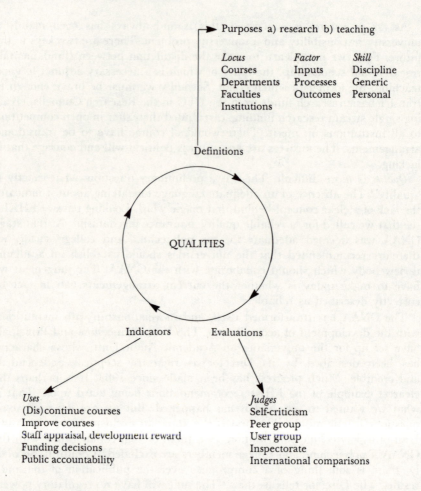

Purposes a) research b) teaching

Locus	*Factor*	*Skill*
Courses	Inputs	Discipline
Departments	Processes	Generic
Faculties	Outcomes	Personal
Institutions		

Definitions

QUALITIES

Indicators   Evaluations

Uses	*Judges*
(Dis)continue courses	Self-criticism
Improve courses	Peer group
Staff appraisal, development reward	User group
Funding decisions	Inspectorate
Public accountability	International comparisons

Figure 1 Higher Education: a model

purposes in which higher education is involved. Multiple definitions of
qualities relating to purposes will require a variety of evaluations, and a
range of different judges to undertake those evaluations. The evaluations will
provide a range of indicators with multiple uses. When the uses are understood, one returns to the definitions of qualities. It is a continuous circle.

Purposes

The model makes the basic distinction between research and teaching and
then pluralizes these terms; in research distinguishing (at least) between
fundamental research and scholarship; in teaching between the disciplinary
or subject skills, the generic or intellectual skills, and the personal or transferable skills. Different levels of judgement must also be distinguished: the

course, department, faculty, institution. There is also an important distinction to be made between inputs, processes and outcomes. In recent years we have come to recognize that outcomes are considerably more important than inputs, however difficult they may be to evaluate. Interest has also grown in the generic and personal skills, though they are as yet inadequately defined and understood.

Judges

Self-criticism must come first, but other judges are also needed – both peer-group and user-group assessment, an external inspectorate (HMI, CNAA, BTEC and the new AAU), and international comparisons.

Indicators

These may be used to continue, or discontinue, courses. But it is more common to use quality-indicators to improve courses. Similarly, staff appraisal may be undertaken for the purpose of rewarding, promoting (or dismissing) staff; but it can also be used to help staff improve the quality of teaching. Sometimes quality indicators determine funding decisions. They are also needed for the fundamental purpose of providing accountability to parliament and the public.

The model may be summed up in the following sentence: 'A diversity of functions requires a variety of qualities.' Higher education has diversity of functions. It must start to recognize a variety of qualities: not *quality* but *qualities*.

Quality evaluation

There is a paradox in quality assurance. The more important quality assurance is seen to be by society at large, the more necessary it is to place the primary responsibility for proper accountability upon the institution and its own academic staff. In the last ten years the public, the government and employers have taken a greater and greater interest in the quality of higher education; higher education should recognize clearly that the primary responsibility for giving an account of its quality lies with the self-critical academic group and self-critical institution. While external forces require accountability, self-regulation should be the basis of quality assurance, with higher education institutions making themselves responsible for offering their own definitions of relevant qualities.

Good quality assurance should be explicit, assessed, with the results known, and their significance 'promoted'. Serious concern about quality is itself probably the best quality indicator there is. An institution that can show itself to be seriously concerned about its own quality is almost by definition likely to be a high quality institution. An institution that refuses to discuss the question is suspect.

In the evaluation of quality it is rarely wise to rely on a single measure or one judge. Good practice normally requires multiple evaluations. And, while quality evaluation in higher education is now seen as an internal responsibility, it is unlikely to be achieved successfully without external contributions.

There are at least three different kinds of relativities which bear on the evaluation of qualities. First, it must be relative to purpose. Second, it is normally relative to last year. We are looking for improvement over time. And third, for some purposes it has to be relative to other providers. These three kinds of relativity are discrete. It is a mistake to confuse them. Similarly there is a diversity of uses for quality indicators. It is important to be clear about how they are going to be used before measurement or judgement begins. The basic use of quality indicators is to promote quality itself.

Funding

It is all very well to know that one course is better or weaker than another, but what is to be done when that is known? Do you reinforce success by diverting money towards the high quality course or do you try to remedy failure by investing more in the weaker course in order to bring it up to standard? Of course the answer is that sometimes you should do one and sometimes the other. There is no mechanical relationship between a relative quality judgement and a funding decision, or there shouldn't be.

Looking forward

Many changes are going to take place over the next ten years. What are they and what will quality issues look like in the light of the changes? The FHE2 seminar foresaw the ending of the binary distinction, much wider participation, new modes of funding and new sources of funding, a solution to the research problem, the European Community and Brussels beginning to take the lead in post-sixteen education and training and, finally, recognition of the continuity of post-compulsory education and training and the principles of lifelong learning. The old binary divide will give way to the new frontier between further and higher education. We shall see the disintegration of watertight courses and watertight higher educational institutions. While we still need to talk about our work in terms of courses and institutions, having no other language, yet with credit accumulation and transfer, with part-time and mixed mode study and with institutions like the Open University (many of whose key members of staff work for other institutions at the same time), the watertight institution and the watertight course are already beginning to be something of an anachronism.

An important question arises at this point. What does the BA (or first degree) certify? One of the approaches to quality must be to answer a question like that. Can we say of all our students, when they are successful in their first degree, that they are competent to make judgements in complex matters, that they have the capability of learning, independently of their teacher and that they have suitability for positions of responsibility and/or leadership in our society? I doubt it. But we need to be able to answer society's question: what is higher about higher education?

Of all the critical issues for the future the most important will be the quality of teaching and learning. That means – let me spell it out – that our concern for the quality of research, our concern for the quality of management in our institutions, our concern for the quality of the environment that we offer our students, will all take second place in the next ten years – except where these issues bear upon and feed into the quality of teaching and learning. *This* will be the major issue.

The seminar recognized that the development of National Vocational Qualifications, the Enterprise in Higher Education initiative and other similar pressures will move attention away from input measures and bring outcomes more sharply into focus. Pauline Perry states that: 'what the student knows, understands and is able to do, is the only legitimate object of the measurement of teaching quality'. I am content with that sentence, but it is a challenge to higher education. We have to consider what I call enablement. What is it that we enable our students to know, to understand, to do? We have to ask what has been gained from a degree course. If we are going to assure quality and be answerable to society we must provide some answers to these questions. Success in this enterprise might mean that quality is no longer the first item on the agenda for the next SRHE/Leverhulme enquiry in ten years time.

Trying to sum up what I see as the main issues in the debate in one recommendation, I draw upon a recent report for which I was responsible:

> That each institution of higher education should review its educational objectives and programme of courses in consultation with users – the students and employers – to ensure that they: a) are attractive, rigorous and enabling; b) provide an appropriate balance of subject skills and knowledge, general conceptual skills, personal transferable skills and appropriate attitudes; c) added value and fitness for purpose to every student. (Ball 1990, p. 7)

Finally, we should consider the system as a whole. Discussion is generally focused on the course or institution, but not on the qualities of the system of higher education. I would say three provocative things about that. A higher educational system that fails to provide the quantity and quality of teachers and engineers its society requires is not a system that we can be satisfied with. A higher education system that is not yet providing for all who are able to benefit from, and who wish for, higher education is not a system that we can be satisfied with. A higher education system which cannot explain what the first degree certifies for all students is not a system that we can be satisfied with.

12

Access, Quality and Governance: One Institution's Struggle for Progress

Tessa Blackstone

Introduction

This chapter is a case study of one university institution's attempt between 1987 and 1990 to improve access, to enhance quality and to create more cost effective and efficient governance. As such it aims to bring together and illustrate some of the individual themes discussed by other contributors to this book in the context of one institution's battle to survive in a hostile climate. In certain respects Birkbeck College is atypical, because over 90 per cent of its students are studying part-time in the evening, for which they pay fees out of taxed income. However, the problems it faces in relation to the book's themes are similar to those of other places. It is desperately short of money. It would like to expand but cannot do so without further government funding. There is an incessant battle to increase income and save on expenditure. What follows is a personal account of how Birkbeck has tried to respond to new challenges and maintain the momentum with respect to innovation and change, at the same time as reducing its unit costs and becoming more efficient. The story is told from my perspective as the head of the institution; others might see things differently. The one advantage those holding the top job have is a perspective of the whole institution and its needs without any vested interest in some part of it.

True to normal university practice I was appointed as Master of Birkbeck over a year before the post became vacant. I knew at the time that the College faced a financial crisis as a result of a UGC decision to alter the formula for funding part-time student places. This did not deter me. In other respects the job is one of the most attractive in British higher education. It was a privilege to be invited to head a college with such a powerful mission to provide educational opportunities for adults – a mission which goes back to the 1820s. Moreover the College's looming deficit posed a challenge, even though inheriting a healthy balance would have been hugely preferable.

The first action I took after a year in waiting was to agree with my predecessor and the Chairman of Governors in the summer of 1987 to invite management consultants to undertake a study of the College's financial situation. At the suggestion of the Chairman of Governors the City Corporation was approached and asked if they could pay for the study. The Corporation had for many years been represented on the College's governing body and, with the help of the governor concerned, the Corporation's agreement to pay was obtained. The study was done by Deloitte's, who produced a thorough and well documented report with the help of a number of senior staff at the College. It is possible that a similar report could have been produced internally. The advantage of employing management consultants was that it provided an independent assessment which could be made available to the University of London and to the UGC and, by dint of being independent, would carry more weight. Deloitte's conclusion was that 'Birkbeck's financial situation is extremely severe and not of its own making. Whatever course is adopted in response will require the co-operation and support of outside bodies. The solution lies outside Birkbeck's own control.'

The solution proposed was that Birkbeck should focus on increasing its income rather than relying mainly on cutting expenditure. The consultants took the view that the College was already run on a shoestring and that the scope for savings was very limited, although they indicated a few areas where they thought some savings might be possible. The main method identified for increasing income was to ask the UGC for 300 additional full-time equivalent funded student places. As long as the College accommodated the extra students without any increases in staff or space, the extra recurrent grant from the UGC and fees from students would go a long way towards resolving the financial crisis.

The consultants did not support the view held by some of the College's staff that the new equivalence ratios for part-time students of 0.77:1 for research students, 0.5:1 for Master's students, and 0.75:1 for undergraduates could be regarded as unreasonable. However, they did think the 26 per cent decline in grant funding the new ratios entailed – a decline which was taking place over a very short period – would be almost impossible to accommodate. They agreed that the College's commitments to its existing students and the virtually fixed nature of its staffing and many of its other costs made such a rapid adjustment totally unrealistic. The College had been saying this for some time to both the UGC and the University of London. The only concession it had succeeded in wringing out of the UGC was a change in the proposed equivalence rate for undergraduates from 0.5 to 0.75. Since it takes only one year more to complete a BA or BSc on a part-time basis at Birkbeck than a conventional full-time first degree elsewhere, 0.75 was clearly a more appropriate ratio than 0.5, which would have been reasonable only if it had taken twice as long. All the College had obtained from the University of London was a loan of £250,000 to help it over the transitional period.

In fact both the UGC and the University had for some months played the game of passing the buck to each other on Birkbeck's financial problems.

This left Birkbeck sitting in the middle increasingly frustrated, until eventually it appealed to the government. In October 1986 a delegation went to see Kenneth Baker, the then Secretary of State for Education and Science. He immediately and with some justice passed the buck back to the UGC and the University. With some justice, except in one respect. The government's policy was, and still is, that part-time students, however poor they are, must pay tuition fees out of taxed income. Full-time students, however rich they are, have their fees paid by their local authorities.

In order to ensure that students from a wide range of backgrounds and income groups had access to Birkbeck courses, and in order to maintain demand for its courses, the College had for many years tried to keep its fees at a fairly low level. Indeed its fees were substantially below the pro rata to full-time fees figure, which the UGC assumed was being charged when making its financial calculations about Birkbeck. This meant, as Deloitte's was to point out, that the College's income was way below that of other institutions. In fact what had happened in the past was that the relatively generous equivalence ratios for part-time to full-time students had made up for, and indeed masked, the loss of income on the fees side.

The Secretary of State was not prepared to change the government's policy on charging fees for part-time courses in order to resolve Birkbeck's financial problems. This left Birkbeck looking for a solution, at least in the short term, through increased funding from the UGC or the University of London, along with any savings it could make. And that solution was provided by Deloitte's recommendations. A request for an extra 300 full-time equivalent students was put to the UGC and accepted. The College put forward a plan for recruiting an extra 500 individuals (making up the 300 fte's) across a wide range of disciplines, over a period of two years. There were to be no concomitant increases in staff; indeed there were to be staff reductions agreed by a Committee, which preceded the Deloitte's review and was chaired by a previous governor of the College, Sir Barney Hayhoe, whose remit was to restructure the College in the interests of greater efficiency and making savings.

The UGC's acceptance of these plans meant the College need no longer fear closure. Until the rescue plan was accepted this seemed a real possibility because of the huge accumulated deficit the College faced. However, although it would clearly survive, the College's problems were not yet over. It faced falling applications for many its courses, part of which was probably due to what might be described as 'planning blight'. Stories in the press about impending bankrupty and closure were putting off potential students. In those circumstances recruiting 500 extra students looked as if it would be a struggle. Even with the extra recurrent grant and fees the new students would bring in, the College would not be out of its financial difficulties because of the deficit it had already accumulated and because it had exhausted its reserves. Many of its staff were becoming demoralized. The College's overall research rating was below the national average, and considerably below the average of the University of London. In these circumstances there was a danger both of a downward spiral of loss of confidence on the part of staff and students, and of a static and unimaginative approach to teaching and research with no funds to finance new developments. To prevent this happening it was vitally important to establish through positive leadership from the top that the College could enhance its reputation and emerge as a stronger institution out of the trough into which it had declined.

Access

Increasing student numbers required considering questions of access. The College had already abandoned a two A level entry requirement for undergraduates and was slowly increasing the proportion of new entrants without traditional qualifications. However, it had shifted towards more and more Master's degree students, so that by 1987 postgraduates constituted more than half of the College's student population. It was essential to stop this trend continuing. Unless this happened the College's traditional role of providing a second chance to those who had missed going to university at the conventional age would have been much diminished. The chance to provide first-time access to higher education for substantial numbers of Londoners and others in the South East would be lost. It was agreed in the College that the proportion of postgraduate students should not exceed 50 per cent of the total. As a consequence academic planning focused on trying to increase undergraduate numbers, and targets were set to try to achieve this.

In her contribution to this volume Elizabeth Reid sets out the goals of what she calls the 'accessible institution'. An institution such as Birkbeck, which is dedicated to mature, part-time students, has already embraced many of these goals. However, financial constraints mean that some highly desirable targets, which will help *widen* access as well as *increase* access, are unachievable. For example, facilities are seriously inadequate for physically disabled students. There is a less than full data base on both applicants and students actually admitted. For instance there is no information about the social origins of students, their current incomes or their ethnic status. All this information is needed if there is to be proper monitoring of progress in widening access. There are also no funds for going out into the community to provide educational advice and counselling on what is available, as Reid recommends.

It is easier to make progress on those aspects of better access where there are few costs. More flexible course structures can be introduced without the need for much extra funding. There is, however, a need to persuade academic staff who are committed to more traditional structures to adapt. At Birkbeck a number of new inter-disciplinary courses have been introduced in the sciences, humanities and social sciences. These courses, which allow students to combine two or three related subjects, have proved to be immensely popular. It is not our experience that mature students generally prefer single-subject honours degrees, as one participant at the FHE2 seminar claimed. Progress has also been made in allowing credit accumulation and transfer. On a number of courses it is also possible to leave after two years or more with a College Certificate or Diploma. Creating greater flexibility by allowing different modes of attendance and switching from one to the other is regrettably not yet possible in an institution where undergraduate courses are only taught in the evening. Instead students wanting to change to a full-time course taught in the day can be advised about how to transfer to another institution taking credits with them; or students wishing to transfer from full-time courses to a part-time Birkbeck course can wherever possible receive credits for what they have already done.

An open admissions policy should, according to Reid, include the targeting of under-represented groups. Birkbeck already had a higher proportion of women than men amongst its undergraduates: because so many more women than men miss out at the conventional age for higher education, it would have been an unforgivable failure were this not the case. Therefore, because of the slight preponderance of women over men, it has not been considered necessary to target them at the recruitment stage. What is essential, however, is to provide childcare facilities in the evening to support single parents, most of whom will be women, and others whose partners cannot always care for the children between 5 and 10 p.m. The College provides an evening nursery in a cost-effective way by making use of premises for this purpose vacated by the neighbouring Institute of Education in the evening.

The other important groups which are under-represented generally are the ethnic minorities. Since there are large Black and Asian communities in Inner London, it should be part of Birkbeck's mission in widening access to try to target these communities. One of the characteristics of Birkbeck recruitment is that much of it is by word of mouth. A student tells his or her friends about the College and its courses. Nothing should be done to discourage this; indeed students are asked to encourage friends who are interested and likely to benefit to apply. Advertising courses is expensive and can only be done on a small scale; spreading the word about courses available is cheap. However, efforts must be and are being made to inform potential students who are unlikely to have friends in the College about what is on offer. One approach has been to place articles about Black or Asian students already at the College in the ethnic press. Role models of success of this kind can prove helpful. Certainly the proportion of students from the ethnic minorities is now increasing at Birkbeck.

The College through its Extra-Mural Centre would also like to mount a network of access courses around London, and in particular in areas of high ethnic minority population. Again this is difficult to do without funding. There are no resources to provide the skilled, specialized staff necessary. Such courses would be particularly useful if they focused on preparing students for courses in the sciences and mathematics, where recruitment is considerably more difficult than in the arts and humanities.

One other issue, which relates to access and which is of particular concern to any institution with large numbers of older part-time students, is wastage rates. It is inevitable that more students will drop out when trying to combine a job with study than when studying full-time. The sacrifices which have to be made are considerable, and some students find the pressures too great to continue. In order to minimize drop-out there must be good pastoral care delivered by understanding and supportive academic staff, who help students through a difficult patch. Peer group support is also important, and is more readily available in an institution such as Birkbeck where all the students are in a similar situation. However, good specialized counselling services are also important. At Birkbeck these are provided through the students' union and by the registry, which focuses in particular on advising students in financial difficulty, who are in danger of dropping out because they are unable to pay their fees and other expenses associated with their studies, such as travel and books. Poorer students and those without conventional academic qualifications, in other words those recruited as a result of policies to widen access, are most at risk. To balance its books the College has had to raise fees each year for the past three years well above inflation. Whilst demand for the College's courses has not been jeopardized by this policy, students on low incomes and/or with several dependants may find it is the straw that breaks the camel's back. To prevent drop-out for this reason the College needs to provide the finance for a larger 'hardship fund' to help these students survive. This also means more staff time to process and check applications for help. It is easy for Ministers to exhort us, as they have done, to charge much higher fees and redistribute some of the income collected to those who cannot afford to pay. This ignores the considerable administrative costs entailed and the unwillingness of some people to become, as they see it, the recipients of charity.

Quality

Turning from questions of access to quality, what can an institution do to enhance the quality of its provision when it is faced with the need to increase its student numbers substantially whilst cutting its staff numbers in order to survive? Staff–student ratios, which had not looked particularly generous under the old equivalence ratios for part-time students, suddenly appeared very favourable. This meant academic departments making substantial adjustments, and in reality having far more students for a given number of staff than they had been used to before. It meant teaching larger groups, which does not necessarily mean a loss of quality, and in some cases having less time for teaching preparation or research, either of which might mean loss of quality. Action was taken to rationalize the teaching of various courses. It is possible in higher education to over-teach. In such cases staff have too little confidence in students' ability to learn on their own, indeed they may damage students' capacity to do so by over-providing lectures, classes, seminars and laboratory demonstrations. This certainly was not the general rule at Birkbeck, but there was some evidence that it was happening in a few departments.

The main form that rationalization has taken has been to rethink the structure of some courses, so that parts of them may be jointly taught with other courses, particularly at MA and MSc level. In highly specialized options there has been some increase in joint teaching of final-year under-graduates and Master's students. Devices of this kind help to reduce the hours academics spend teaching very small groups and mean they can continue to commit considerable time to either teaching preparation or research – vital tasks in ensuring quality. In stating this I am not suggesting that continuing downward pressure on staff–student ratios can be handled in this way without affecting quality. There is a limit to how far courses can be rationalized by these means. Moreover, good courses will entail some tutorial teaching and individual counselling which cannot be properly sustained with ever-increasing numbers and no growth in staff, not to mention the extra pressures of admissions work or examining.

In FHE1 a strong case was made for moving away from highly specialized single-subject honours degrees, and I have already made reference to Birk-beck pursuing this policy through the introduction of a number of inter-disciplinary courses. Allowing students to pursue rather broader academic interests need in no way reduce quality, a fact that seems to have escaped Mrs Thatcher, when as Prime Minister she stood in the way of A level reform, apparently believing broadening would diminish standards. At Birk-beck there are now inter-disciplinary degrees in humanities (mainly focusing on language, literature and cultural studies), in politics, philosophy and history, in economic and social policy, in mathematics, statistics and compu-ter science, and in cognitive studies (covering psychology, philosophy and computer science), to name but a few.

In her chapter Pauline Perry argues that indices of quality should rest on measures of student achievement, *including their acceptability by employers*, as well as on the institutional measures taken to maximize the use of limited resources. Both of these might raise eyebrows, in some academic circles, as valid measures of quality. But whilst higher education is clearly about more than preparing students for employment, it does not seem outrageous to suggest that one criterion of quality might include the acceptability of new graduates to employers.

Partly with this in mind, Birkbeck has not just increased the number of inter-disciplinary degrees, it has also successfully bid for funding from the Training Enterprise and Education Directorate of the Department of Em-ployment, under the Enterprise in Higher Education programme. In doing so staff have had to think about the content of their courses and their teaching methods in a way which ought to enhance students' achievement and thereby quality. The programme will provide greater focus than in the past on personal transferable skills. These will include: first, the ability to perceive, analyse and solve complex issues and problems, setting goals, managing resources within constraints and evaluating results; second, the ability to use information and to communicate effectively, including oral, written and visual presentation; and third, the ability to work individually and with others, self-knowledge, and leadership, co-operation, teamwork and task-sharing. There will be an increased emphasis on self-assessment and active forms of teaching and learning, as well as close teaching links with local employers in the public, private, and voluntary sectors. One spin-off should be greater scope to tap the considerable experience and expertise mature students bring with them, and through interaction with other students in classes and seminars to ensure that these are shared.

Judgements of quality in relation to academic institutions should not just be about the output of teaching. Research outputs must be considered too. Birkbeck has had a long history of excellence in its research contribution in a number of fields. Its great names include J. D. Bernal in crystallography, Nikolaus Pevsner in the history of art and more recently Eric Hobsbawm in economic history. However, when the UGC undertook its first research selectivity exercise in 1985 no Birkbeck department received a top rating, though there were a number in the second highest category, and the overall position of the College in the league table was well down in the bottom half.

It was essential to improve on this: first, to ensure that our students, especially our many graduate students, were being taught by people at the frontiers of their subjects; second, to retain our most able staff and to attract able new people; and third, to secure the higher funding associated with positive research ratings. The morale of many existing staff was certainly likely to be affected, were there to be any further decline in the College's research reputation. All departments were asked to work to improve their research ratings, and a mixture of carrots and sticks was employed to achieve this. Consequently there was a dramatic improvement in research grant and research contract income as well as improved publication rates in many subjects. As a result in the second selectivity exercise in 1989 the College moved into the top half of the league table. Only three departments had below average ratings, with two departments obtaining top ratings. Since nearly all Birkbeck's departments are small and the UFC's procedures for judging research quality tend to favour larger departments, this was a considerable achievement.

Whether it can be improved on again, and whether the successful reforms introduced on the teaching side can be maintained, depends crucially on the quality of the inputs. Against the resource constraints the College faces, it has been a constant battle to maintain standards of equipment, computing facilities and the library. The environment in which many of our staff and students have to work is unsatisfactory. Lecture halls, classrooms and laboratories are in many cases dingy and overcrowded. There is insufficient funding to carry out the required maintenance, and all too little for capital improvements. Much more intensive use is now made of all accommodation. That is as it should be, but it costs more on the recurrent side to use buildings so intensively. The College has abandoned any attempts to cater for research in its own library: staff and research students must go elsewhere. It is becoming increasingly difficult for the library to meet the needs of students even with respect to teaching, because of lack of resources. It is not possible to achieve the goal of ensuring that all students, including those studying the arts and humanities, become computer literate because the facilities are not there. Any improvement in funding must mean high priority being attached to improving the library and providing more computers. Unless this happens quality will decline relative to other institutions.

By far the most important input concerns staff. Improving quality means above all more dedicated, able and talented staff, and it is a little surprising that discussion of quality often makes little reference to this fact. Birkbeck has been singularly lucky in the dedication and loyalty of its staff. Its unique characteristics as the only university institution dedicated to teaching mature students part-time make it special to those who work in it. However, any institution has some staff who do not achieve what is expected of them. The UFC's early retirement scheme has been used to encourage some people in this category to go. Schemes for supporting probationers have been implemented and a tougher line has been taken with those not performing adequately. Considerable effort must be put into the recruitment of new staff. In the last three years no advertised professorial post has been filled by anyone without at least a national reputation in his or her field. This has been achieved by seeking out people and persuading them to apply rather than waiting for applications to come in. Talented young people are still coming forward to enter university teaching in spite of the decline in pay and working conditions, though recruitment of able people is difficult in some subjects. Many more of them are women than in the past; research findings suggest that women are rather less concerned about pay than men in making occupational choices, although this may change. Birkbeck has managed to recruit a number of very talented lecturers over the last three years, 40 per cent of whom are women. This influx of new talent is vital to maintain and indeed improve quality.

Governance

Many of the issues concerning governance revolve round the relationship between the government, the national funding bodies and higher education institutions. In a case study of this kind it would not be appropriate to go into these macro questions. This section will therefore be briefer than the two which precede it, and will concentrate solely on some micro issues of institutional governance. William Stubbs refers in his chapter on governance to a greater emphasis in the last decade on management skills in the running of institutions. He mentions strategic plans and performance indicators. Clearly both academic and financial planning have become more important in a context where resources are scarce and funding less generous. It is not just good management that is needed to obtain value for money and to allocate resources fairly on the basis of performance. Leadership skills are equally necessary in identifying priorities and setting targets and ensuring they are implemented and achieved and in projecting the institution and its mission to the external world.

At Birkbeck there have been five main tasks to accomplish to achieve a well-managed institution. The College needed:

1. A new structure with larger units than the many small departments for the purposes of resource allocation and financial administration.
2. Improved financial management, including better budgeting, the elimination of overspending and clear criteria for the allocation of resources through formula funding.
3. A streamlined system of decision-making through fewer and smaller committees.
4. A more professional administration with, for example more efficient management of accommodation and maintenance of buildings, up-to-date personnel policies including equal opportunities, the provision of regular financial information and the computerization of records.
5. Revisions to the Charter and Statutes to alter the composition of the Governing Body to provide more lay members and to take into account other external changes such as the 1988 Education Reform Act.

Considerable progress has been made in achieving these tasks although the revision of the Charter and Statutes is not yet complete and there is always room for further improvement in administrative procedures. Examples of progress include the reorganization of the College into eight resource centres, groupings of related departments, on the recommendation of the Hayhoe Committee, to which reference has already been made. After a review of the operation of the system after two years, a further reorganization took place reducing the resource centres to six. Each resource centre is headed by a senior academic, appointed for five years. They form the College's senior management team along with the Master, the Vice-Master and the Secretary, Registrar and Finance Secretary. The committee structure has been simplified so that nearly all of the College's business is undertaken through the work of six main committees. Some duplication of business still exists between committees but it has been greatly reduced. It is vital to minimize the time academics have to spend in committee meetings, so that they can pursue their central tasks of teaching and research.

Financial controls are operated much more strictly than in the past. Over-spending is penalized. Some budgets have been devolved, and further moves in this direction are being contemplated. *Ad hoc* deals involving 'slush funds' being doled out to those who put most pressure on the administration are a thing of the past. Formulae based broadly on UFC funding models have been devised to encourage the recruitment of extra students and the seeking of more research income. Research contracts are no longer signed by the College unless significant overheads are obtained. Accommodation has been reorganized and reallocated to make better use of space.

To achieve so much change over a period of three years has taxed many people to their limits. To pretend that it has taken place without conflict and without some people feeling they are worse off than before would be complacent and smug. It has been an immense struggle. There have certainly been times when the academic staff have felt that the management was being too ruthless in its pursuit of efficiency. But most would, I hope, concede that the College had to adapt the way it was managed and governed to a harsher external climate.

In conclusion, what has been achieved so far with respect to access, quality and governance is only a beginning. The next phase of the College's development must be to expand substantially. Only then will it be truly viable in a world of ever more squeezes on the unit of resource. Larger departments can benefit from economies of scale, provide students with a wider range of academic expertise, and extend the range of intellectual discourse for staff. Above all, expansion will open up opportunities for many more mature students who wish to study part-time. The College has made its case as eloquently and forcibly as it can. The decision on whether it will happen lies elsewhere with the University Funding Council. Rejection of Birkbeck's case would, I believe, run counter to the recommendations of FHE1 ten years ago and FHE2 today for greater access to higher education for mature students studying part-time. Turning from Birkbeck to the system as a whole, the incentives for institutions to expand part-time provision at undergraduate level are negligible. A policy to expand part-time places must face up to the fee issue. Differentiating between full- and part-time students taking a first degree should come to an end: as long as full-time students have their fees paid by LEAs so should part-time students. This change would have the effect both of increasing access for individual students and of encouraging institutions to expand part-time provision in a context where fee income is an increasing proportion of total income. I am optimistic enough to hope that a future Secretary of State for Education will be sufficiently farsighted to make this change, and that it will take place sooner rather than later.

Appendix

The Future of Higher Education: A Reassessment
19–21 September 1990: Birkbeck College
List of Participants

Sir Christopher Ball, Royal Society of Arts.
Richard Bird, formerly Under-Secretary, Department of Education and Science.
Baroness Blackstone, Master, Birkbeck College.
Tony Clark, Under-Secretary, Further and Higher Education, Department of Education and Science.
Patrick Coldstream, Director, Council for Industry and Higher Education.
Ngaio Crequer, Education Editor, *The Independent*.
Professor Chris Duke, Department of Continuing Education, University of Warwick.
Colin Flint, Principal, Solihull College of Technology.
Dr Malcolm Frazer, Chief Executive, Council for National Academic Awards.
Dr Oliver Fulton, Director, Institute for Research and Development in Post-Compulsory Education, Lancaster University.
Dorotea Furth, Education Division, Organization for Economic Co-operation and Development, Paris.
Professor Ruth Gee, Director, Edge Hill College of Higher Education.
Dr Arnold Goldman, Academic Staff Development Co-ordinator and Senior Enterprise Adviser, University of Kent.
Professor Christine King, Assistant Director, Staffordshire Polytechnic.
Cari Loder, Research Officer, Institute of Education, London University.
Karen MacGregor, *Times Higher Education Supplement*.
Gordon McNair, Head of Higher Education Branch, Employment Department, Training Agency.
Professor Andrew McPherson, Director, Centre for Educational Sociology, University of Edinburgh.
Finnbar O'Callaghan, Commission of the European Communities.
Richard Pearson, Deputy Director, Institute of Manpower Studies, University of Sussex.
Pauline Perry, Director, South Bank Polytechnic.
Elizabeth Reid, Deputy Provost, City of London Polytechnic.
Michael Richardson, Pro-Vice-Chancellor (Continuing Education), Open University.
David Robertson, Director of Access Services, Liverpool Polytechnic.

Tom Schuller, Director, Centre for Continuing Education, University of Edinburgh.
Peter Scott, Editor, *Times Higher Education Supplement*.
Michael Shattock, Registrar, University of Warwick.
William Solesbury, Secretary, Economic and Social Research Council.
Dr William Stubbs, Chief Executive, Polytechnics and Colleges Funding Council.
Quentin Thompson, Associate Director, Coopers and Lybrand Deloitte.
Sir Aubrey Trotman-Dickenson, Principal, University College, Cardiff.
Diana Warwick, General Secretary, Association of University Teachers.
Dr Susan Weil, Chair, Society for Research into Higher Education; Associate Director, Higher Education for Capability, RSA.
Professor Gareth Williams, Institute of Education, London University.
Peter Williams, Director Designate, CVCP Academic Audit Unit.

References

Astin, A. (1983). 'Strengthening transfer programs' in G. Vaughan and Associates, *Issues for Community College Leaders in a New Era*. San Francisco: Jossey-Bass, pp. 122–38.

Baker, K. (1988). Letter to Chairman, Polytechnics and Colleges Funding Council.

Baker, K. (1989). 'Higher education – 25 years on'. Speech at Lancaster University, 5 January. London: Department of Education and Science.

Ball, Sir C. (1985). *Fitness for Purpose: Essays in Higher Education*. Guildford: SRHE and NFER-Nelson.

Ball, Sir C. (1990). *More Means Different: Widening Access to Higher Education*. London: Royal Society for the Encouragement of Arts, Manufactures and Commerce.

Becher, T. (1990). *Academic Tribes and Territories*. Milton Keynes: SRHE/Open University Press.

Bok, D. (1986). *Higher Learning*. Boston: Harvard University Press.

Brint, S. and Karabel, J. (1989). *The Diverted Dream: Community Colleges and the Promise of Educational Opportunity in America, 1900–1985*. New York: Oxford University Press.

British Petroleum (1989). *Aiming for a College Education*. London: BP Educational Service.

Burnhill, P., Garner, C.L. and McPherson, A.F. (1990). 'Parental education, social class and entry to higher education', *Journal of the Royal Statistical Society, Series A* **153**: 233–48.

CHE (1963). Committee on Higher Education *Report*. London: HMSO, Cmnd 2154.

CSO (1990). Central Statistical Office, *Regional Trends 25*. London: HMSO.

CVCP (1985). *Report of the Steering Committee for Efficiency Studies in Universities (Jarratt Report)*. London: CVCP.

CVCP/CNAA (1989, 1990). *Access Courses to Higher Education: a framework of national arrangements for recognition* **(1), (2), (3)**. London: CNAA.

Davie, G. (1986). *The Crisis of the Democratic Intellect*. Edinburgh: Polygon.

DES (1978). *Higher Education into the 1990s*. London: Department of Education and Science.

DES (1984). *Technical Report to DES Report on Education Number 100*. London: Department of Education and Science (mimeo).

DES (1985). *The Development of Higher Education into the 1990s*. London: HMSO, Cm. 9524.

DES (1986). *Projections of Demand for Higher Education in Great Britain 1986–2000*. London: Department of Education and Science.

DES (1987). *Higher Education: Meeting the Challenge*. London: HMSO, Cm. 114.

DES (1988a). 'Student numbers in higher education – Great Britain 1975– 1986', *Statistical Bulletin 8/88*. London: Department of Education and Science.

DES (1988b). *Advancing A levels*. London: HMSO.

DES (1989a). *The English Polytechnics: An HMI Commentary*. London: HMSO.

DES (1989b). *Report by HM Inspectors on the Widening of Access to Higher Education*. London: Department of Education and Science.

DES (1990a). Personal communication of unpublished figures.

DES (1990b). 'Student numbers in higher education – Great Britain 1975–1988', *Statistical Bulletin 11/90*. London: Department of Education and Science.

DES (1991a). *Education and Training for the 21st Century*. London: HMSO, Cm. 1536.

DES (1991b). *Higher Education: A New Framework*. London: HMSO, Cm. 1541.

Duffy, M. (1990). 'The changing relationship between schools and higher education', in G. Parry and C. Wake (eds), *Access and Alternative Futures for Higher Education*. London: Hodder and Stoughton, pp. 98–112.

Duke, C. (1989). 'Creating the Accessible Institution', in O. Fulton (ed.), *Access and Institutional Change*. Milton Keynes: SRHE/Open University Press.

Farrant, J.H. (1981). 'Trends in admissions', in O. Fulton (ed.) (1981b), *Access to Higher Education*. Guildford: SRHE, pp. 42–88.

Finegold, D., Keep, E., Miliband, D., Raffe, D., Spours, K. and Young, M. (1990). *A British 'Baccalauréat': Ending the Division Between Education and Training*. Education and Training Paper 1. London: Institute for Public Policy Research.

Fulton, O. (1981a). 'Principles and policies', in O. Fulton (ed.) (1981b), *Access to Higher Education*. Guildford: SRHE, pp. 5–41.

Fulton, O. (ed.) (1981b). *Access to Higher Education*. Guildford: SRHE.

Fulton, O. (ed.) (1989). *Access and Institutional Change*. Milton Keynes: SRHE/Open University Press.

Fulton, O. and Ellwood, S. (1989). *Admissions to Higher Education: Policy and Practice*. Sheffield: The Training Agency.

Glennerster, H. and Low, W. (1991). 'Education and the welfare state: does it add up?' in J. Hills. (ed.), *The State of Welfare: The Welfare State in Britain since 1974*. Oxford: Clarendon Press, pp. 28–77.

Higginson, G. (1990). 'A levels and the future', in G. Parry and C. Wake (eds), *Access and Alternative Futures for Higher Education*. London: Hodder and Stoughton, pp. 77–97.

House of Commons (1980). *Fifth Report by the Select Committee on Education, Science and Arts*. London: HMSO, HC 787–1.

House of Commons (1990a). *House of Commons Committee of Public Accounts First Report – Financial Problems at Universities*, 15 January. London: HMSO.

House of Commons (1990b). Treasury Minute on the Thirty Third to Thirty Sixth Reports from the Committee of Public Accounts 1989–1990. London: HMSO, Cmnd 1323.

Interdepartmental Review (1990). *Highly Qualified People: Supply and Demand*. London: HMSO.

Jesson, D. and Gray, J. (1990). 'Access, entry and potential demand for higher education amongst 18–19 year olds in England and Wales', Research and Development 60, *Youth Cohort Series 12*. Sheffield: The Training Agency.

Leiven, M. (1989). 'Access courses after ten years: a review', *Higher Education Quarterly* **43**: 160–75.

Lindley, R. (ed.) (1981). *Higher Education and the Labour Market*. Guildford: SRHE.

MacGregor, J. (1990). '*The Future of Higher Education*'. The Broomfield Memorial Lecture given at Portsmouth Polytechnic, 6 June. London: Department of Education and Science.

McPherson, A.F., Raffe, D. and Robertson, C. (1990). *Highers and Higher Education*. Edinburgh: Association of University Teachers.

Moser, Sir C. (1990). *Our Need for an Informed Society*. London: Presidential Address to the British Association for the Advancement of Science.

National Advisory Body (1988). *Action for Access*. London: NAB.

Parry, G. and Wake, C. (eds) (1990). *Access and Alternative Futures* for *Higher Education*. London: Hodder and Stoughton.

Paterson, L. (forthcoming). *The Influence of Opportunity on Aspirations, amongst Prospective University Entrants from Scottish Schools 1970–1988*. Edinburgh: University of Edinburgh Centre for Educational Sociology (mimeo).

Pippard, A.B. (1972). 'The structure of a morally committed university' in J. Lawlor (ed.), *Higher Education: Patterns of Change in the 1970s*. London: Routledge and Kegan Paul, pp. 67–87.

Polytechnics and Colleges Funding Council (PCFC) (1990a). *A Guide to the Aims and Objectives of the Council and the Polytechnics and Colleges it funds*. London: PCFC.

Polytechnics and Colleges Funding Council (PCFC) (1990b). *Performance Indicators*. Report of a Committee of Enquiry chaired by Mr Alfred Morris. London: PCFC.

Raffe, D. (1991). 'Scotland v. England: The place of "home internationals" in comparative research' in P. Ryan (ed.), *International Comparisons of Vocational Education and Training*. Lewes: Falmer.

Redpath, R. and Harvey, B. (1987). *Young People's Intentions to Enter Higher Education*. London: HMSO.

Robbins, L. (1963). *Report of the Committee on Higher Education*. London: HMSO, Cmnd 2154.

Robbins, L. (1980). *Higher Education Revisited*. London: Macmillan.

Rudd, E. (1987). 'The educational qualifications and social class of the parents of undergraduates entering British universities in 1984', *Journal of the Royal Statistical Society, Series A* **150**: 346–72.

Sargant, N. (1990). 'Access and the media' in G. Parry and C. Wake (eds), *Access and Alternative Futures for Higher Education*. London: Hodder and Stoughton, pp. 181–207.

Schuller, T., Tight, M., and Weil, S. (1988). 'Continuing education and the redrawing of boundaries', *Higher Education Quarterly* **43**(4): 335–52.

Schuller, T. (1990). 'The exploding community? The university idea and the smashing of the academic atom', *Oxford Review of Education* **16**(1): 3–14.

Schuller, T. and Walker, A. (1990). *The Time of Our Life: Education, Employment and the Third Age*. London: Institute for Public Policy Research.

SEAC (1990). Consultation on the draft principles for GCE Advanced Supplementary and Advanced examinations. London: School Examinations and Assessment Council (mimeo).

SED (1990a). 'Higher education projections for Scotland', *Statistical Bulletin* **8/J1/ 1990**. Edinburgh: Scottish Education Department.

SED (1990b). 'Scottish higher education statistics', *Statistical Bulletin* **12/J2/1990**. Edinburgh: Scottish Education Department.

Shattock, M. (ed.) (1983). *Structure and Governance in Higher Education*. Guildford: SRHE.

Smithers, A. and Robinson, P. (1989). *Increasing Participation in Higher Education*. London: British Petroleum International.

SOED (1991). *Access and Opportunity: A Strategy for Education and Training*. London: HMSO, Cm. 1530.

SRHE-Leverhulme (1983). *Excellence in Diversity*. Guildford: SRHE.

Tight, M. (1989). 'The ideology of higher education', in O. Fulton (ed.), *Access and Institutional Change*. Milton Keynes: SRHE/Open University Press, pp. 85–98.

Tight, M. (1991). *Higher Education: A Part-time Perspective*. Milton Keynes: SRHE/Open University Press.

Tolley, G. (1990). 'Enterprise, scholars and students', in G. Parry and C. Wake (eds), *Access and Alternative Futures for Higher Education*. London: Hodder and Stoughton, pp. 146–58.

Wagner, L. (1989). 'National policy and institutional development', in O. Fulton (ed.), *Access and Institutional Change*. Milton Keynes: SRHE/Open University Press, pp. 149–62.

Wasser, H. (1990). 'Changes in the European university: from traditional to entrepreneurial', *Higher Education Quarterly* **44**(2): 110–21.

Williams, G. (1983). 'The Leverhulme programme of study into the future of higher education: future prospects', in N. Phillipson (ed.), *Universities, Society and the Future*. Edinburgh: Edinburgh University Press, pp. 236–47.

Williams, G. (1985). 'Survival in a harsh climate', in D. Jaques and J. Richardson (eds), *The Future of Higher Education*. Guildford: SRHE and NFER-Nelson, pp. 55–64.

Williams, G. (1990). *Funding Higher Education: Current Patterns*. Paris: OECD.

Williams, G. and Blackstone, T. (eds) (1983) *Response to Adversity*. Guildford: SRHE.

Williams, G. and Loder, C. (eds) (1991). *Business Funding of Higher Education*. London: Centre for Higher Education Studies.

Williams, G. (1992). *New Funding Mechanisms in Higher Education*. Milton Keynes: Open University Press.

Index

The Society for Research into Higher Education

The Society for Research into Higher Education exists to stimulate and co-ordinate research into all aspects of higher education. It aims to improve the quality of higher education through the encouragement of debate and publication on issues of policy, on the organization and management of higher education institutions, and on the curriculum and teaching methods.

The Society's income is derived from subscriptions, sales of its books and journals, conference fees and grants. It receives no subsidies, and is wholly independent. Its individual members include teachers, researchers, managers and students. Its corporate members are institutions of higher education, research institutes, professional, industrial and governmental bodies. Members are not only from the UK, but from elsewhere in Europe, from America, Canada and Australasia, and it regards its international work as amongst its most important activities.

Under the imprint SRHE & Open University Press, the Society is a specialist publisher of research, having some 30 titles in print. The Editorial Board of the Society's Imprint seeks authoritative research or study in the field. It offers competitive royalties, a highly recognizable format in both hard- and paper-back and the world-wide reputation of the Open University Press.

The Society also publishes *Studies in Higher Education* (three times a year), which is mainly concerned with academic issues, *Higher Education Quarterly* (formerly *Universities Quarterly*), mainly concerned with policy issues, *Abstracts* (three times a year), and SRHE NEWS (four times a year).

The Society holds a major annual conference in December, jointly with an institution of higher education. In 1990, the topic was 'Industry and Higher Education', at and with the University of Surrey. Future conferences include in 1991, 'Research and Higher Education in Europe', with the University of Leicester, in 1992, 'Learning to Effect', with Nottingham Polytechnic, and in 1993, 'Governments and the Higher Education Curriculum' with the University of Sussex. In addition it holds regular seminars and consultations on topics of current interest.

The Society's committees, study groups and branches are run by members. The groups at present include:
Teacher Education Study Group
Continuing Education Group
Staff Development Group
Excellence in Teaching & Learning
Women in Higher Education Group.

Benefits to members

Individual

Individual members receive:

- The NEWS, the Society's publications list, conference details and other material included in mailings.
- Reduced rates for *Studies in Higher Education* (£9.75 per year – full price £72) and *Higher Education Quarterly* (£12.35 per year – full price £43).
- A 35% discount on all Open University Press & SRHE publications.
- Free copies of the Proceedings (or Precedings) – commissioned papers on the theme of the Annual Conference.
- Free copies of *Higher Education Abstracts*.
- Reduced rates for conferences.
- Extensive contacts and scope for facilitating initiatives.
- Reduced reciprocal memberships.

Corporate

Corporate members receive:

- All benefits of individual members, plus
- Free copies of *Studies in Higher Education*.
- Unlimited copies of the Society's publications at reduced rates.
- Special rates for its members, e.g. to the Annual Conference.

Subscriptions August 1991–July 1992

Individual members

standard fee	£ 47
hardship (e.g. unwaged)	£ 22
students and retired	£ 14

Corporate members

a) teaching institutions		
under 1000 students		£170
up to 3000 students		£215
over 3000 students		£320
b) non-teaching institutions	up to	£325
c) industrial/professional bodies	up to	£325

SRHE *Further information*: SRHE at the University, Guildford GU2 5XH, UK
Tel: (0483) 39003 Fax: (0483) 300803
Catalogue: SRHE & Open University Press, Celtic Court, 22 Ballmoor, Buckingham MK18 1XW. Tel: (0280) 823388